The Prophecies of Nostradamus

THE PROPHECIES OF NOSTRADAMUS

David Geddes

CAXTON REFERENCE

This edition published 2000 by Caxton Editions,
20 Bloomsbury Street, London, WC1B 3QA.

Caxton Editions is an imprint of the Caxton Publishing Group.

Printed and bound in India.

CONTENTS

INTRODUCTION

The Legend

Nostradamus is a man of mystery, a man of controversy, a man with many believers and even more sceptics. At the end of the 20th century and the beginning of the 21st, his name is more widely known than during his lifetime in the 16th century. He is, in fact, a legend.

Nostradamus is a legend today and is the subject of innumerable books, studies and translations. Articles regularly appear in newspapers attempting to explain his prophecies which seem to refer to our time. It is an extraordinary fact that his prophecies have been in print continuously for almost 450 years – a record that few works can equal.

Nostradamus was also a legend in his own lifetime. Stories of his ability to foretell the future began to circulate widely. One story told of his meeting with a group of monks as he travelled in Italy. As the monks were passing, he singled out one of them and dropped to his knees in front of him. The monk was of very humble birth and the others were surprised by this act of homage. They were amused when Nostradamus said, 'I must bend my knee before His Holiness'. Forty years later the humble Brother Peretti became Pope Sixtus V and the legend of Nostradamus grew. This man of legend was, in many ways, a mystery to the people of his own time and has continued to mystify and fascinate generations after his death.

The Life

Michel de Nostradamus was born in 1503, within sight of the church in the centre of the town of St Remy de Provence. He was from a Jewish family which had recently converted to Christianity and much of his early education came from Jean de St Remy, his mother's grandfather. The old man fed the boy's hunger for learning and encouraged him to take his education further.

At the age of 14, Michel went to study in Avignon about 12 miles from St Remy. He was already showing a talent for mathematics and a real interest in astrology. Even at this early age he had strong opinions and debated with his teachers the merit of astrology and defended the theory of Copernicus that the earth and the planets rotated around the sun. In 1522, he went to the University of Montpellier to study medicine and there he mixed with some of the greatest thinkers of the day such as Rabelais Montpellier was the source of learning brought by Arab and Jewish scholars from Spain and, in particular, the University encouraged new paths of knowledge, especially in the area of medicine. Michel de Nostradamus easily passed his university examinations in 1525 and soon afterwards his new-found knowledge was urgently required. In the 16th century France was ravaged by outbreaks of bubonic plague and this latest epidemic was so severe that Montpellier University closed down and all members of the medical faculty, including students, left to fight the disease throughout the south of France. For approximately four years Michel followed the path of the epidemic, working ceaselessly in every town until the plague was defeated. He travelled as far as Bordeaux during this time, gaining experience and expanding his knowledge from meeting the many alchemists and doctors engaged in fighting the black death.

In 1529 he returned to the University in Montpellier and he attained his doctorate in medicine. Also at this time he changed his name to the Latinized version and was known henceforth as Nostradamus. He was a professor of medicine at the University until in 1532 he set up a practice in Toulouse. Two years later, he moved to Agen, between

Toulouse and Bordeaux where he established a very successful medical practice. This was a very happy time for Nostradamus as he met and married a beautiful young woman and their son and daughter were born. He also became friends with Julius-Cesar Scaliger, one of the prominent minds of the Renaissance, who introduced him to the local society. This happy period was shattered in 1537 when the plague struck again in Agen and his wife and two children died. His patients lost all confidence in a doctor who could not save his own family and his practice crumbled. Also at this time, Nostradamus was being investigated by the Church over comments which he had made some years previously and he was summoned to appear before the Inquisition in Toulouse. It is small wonder that he quietly left Agen and for the next six years of his life he kept on the move to escape the Inquisition and attempt to put his life together again. He travelled great distances throughout Europe and lived for some time in Sicily. It was during this sad and dangerous time that stories began to circulate about his prophetic gift and the

Nostradamus legend took root. After his years of wandering, Nostradamus settled for a while in Marseilles and set up a practice. During the winter of 1544 devastating floods struck Provence causing terror and death throughout the region. Nostradamus was an exceptional doctor and in 1546 he worked ceaselessly for many months in Aix, the capital of Provence to fight a major outbreak of the plague. Working with an apothecary he produced new medicines and discontinued the traditional bleeding of plague victims. He also advocated stricter hygiene and an improved diet, which proved him to be in the vanguard of medical progress. The people of Aix honoured him and gave him a pension for life. After around nine months in Aix, Nostradamus was called out to fight the plague and other illnesses in Salon and Lyons and then settled in Salon in 1547.

He was to spend the remainder of his life in the attractive town of Salon and it was here that he married again and raised a family of six children. In his first years in Salon, Nostradamus slowly disengaged himself from the world of medicine and became more and more involved in astrology. He believed that during his experience's in combating disease, despairing men and women had pleaded with him to find an explanation for their suffering in the cosmic movement of the stars. He felt that, as he had been granted a second wife, family and happiness, he could finally devote himself to study rather than healing. He created a secret study on the top floor of his house and he set about writing his first predictions. Beginning with predictions in an annual almanac he then embarked on his magnum opus The Prophecies. The fame of his predictions and prophecies spread gaining him the friendship of Queen Catherine de Medici and the Duke and Duchess of Savoy, who became his patrons. In 1564, Nostradamus was visited in his home in Salon by Catherine de Medici and her son, the young King Charles IX and was honoured by the title Counsellor and Physician in Ordinary. By this time Nostradamus was becoming frailer and in 1566 his legendary strong health declined rapidly and he died on 2 July 1566. His wife arranged to have the following epitaph inscribed in his tomb:

Here rest the bones of the illustrious Michel Nostradamus, alone of all mortals judged worthy to record with his near divine pen, under the influence of the stars, the future events of the entire world. He lived 62 years, six months and 17days . He died at Salon in the year 1566. Let not posterity disturb his rest. Anne Ponsorde Gemelle wishes her husband true happiness.

The Prophecies

At the end of his life Nostradamus was concious of the various areas of knowledge in which he had studied amd participated. His life had been fulfilled and he wished to leave legacies appropriate to each sphere of his experience.

To his colleagues in medicine and the apothecaries who had aided hime he left a treatise on different powders and balms for the beauty of skin and face and recipes for various jams as aids to good health. In recognition of the benefits he had received from scholarships he left translations of ancient documents and books. Finally, in gratitude for what life had taught him, he left the ten centuries, which were the heart of his prophecies. These centuries were born out of his nocturnal prophetic calculations and his belief that he could foresee the moments and hours of events.

Does Nostradamus deserve to be taken seriously as a seer and prophet? His writing is very obscure and uses fragments of Latin, Italian, Hebrew, Arabic and Greek as well as

French. The ten centuries set out to span the future history of the world and are written in 1,000 puzzling quatrains or poems of four lines. It is thought that a major reason for the obscurity was that Nostradamus was in constant danger of being branded a magician or heretic by the Church, which could put his work and even his life in jeopardy. The most successful prophecy in his own lifetime predicted the death in a jousting accident of King Henry II of France.

The young lion will defeat the old,
On the field of battle in single combat
His eyes will be pierced through a cage of gold,
Two blows then death cruel death.

Three years after the prophecy the King was indeed killed during a tournament when a splinter of wood penetrated his golden visor and pierced his brain. The crowds called on the Inquisitors to burn Nostradamus and he was saved only by the intervention of Queen Catherine.

The Prophecies of Nostradamus will always be an enigma and he has often been denounced as a fake or a fraud. There is, however, something in the man and his predictions which constantly fascinates and has drawn scholars to study his quatrains down through the ages.

The prophecies begin with a preface which is dedicated to his infant son Cesar. This preface is in a prose style which presages future history and the end of the world, possibly after the year 3,500AD. In our own time, Nostradamus seems to indicate a third world war in the 2020's followed by the Golden Age of Aquarius.

The Centuries are the heart of the prophecies of Nostradamus and what follows is a selection from the total of 1,000 quatrains, illustrating predictions for various stages in the history of the world.

The Centuries

Century I Quatrain 3

When the litter is destroyed by a whirlwind,

And faces concealed by their cloaks,

The republic will be vexed by new people

Then whites and reds will be wrong.

This quatrain describes the storm and upheaval of the French Revolution and the bloody end of the Bourbons, whose badge was the white cockade.

Century I Quatrain 7

> *A late arrival and the act committed,*
>
> *The head wind and letters intercepted ,*
>
> *Fourteen conspiritors in the party,*
>
> *Rousseau will carry out the deed*

In 1894, a French Jewish army officer, Alfred Dreyfuss was wrongly accused of espionage and treason in that he had given secret papers to Germany. The judge in the case was Waldeck Rousseau, who was named in the quatrain and was a known anti-Semite. Dreyfuss had a strong defender in Emile Zola but, in spite of this, Dreyfuss was found guilty and imprisoned on Devil's Island.

In a second trial, Dreyfuss was again found guilty by Rousseau but was then pardoned by President Loubet.

Century I Quatrain 14

> *From people in slavery, songs and requests,*
>
> *The princes and lords are captives in prisons,*
>
> *Fools in the future will take*
>
> *These requests as divine utterances.*

The French Revolution. Nostradamus was seeing the mob in Paris rioting through the streets shouting revolutionary war-cries and perhaps singing the Marseillaise.

This prophecy has also been suggested as describing the Russian Revolution.

Century I Quatrain 16

> *Saturn moving towards Sagittarius,*
>
> *At its highest point,*
>
> *Pest, famine and death from armies,*
>
> *The era comes to its renewal*

This quatrain may be warning of the plague, famines and drought which have afflicted the world in recent years. These dreadful events have affected Africa, Asia, Southern Europe and North America.

He also appears to be referring to the vastly increased world-wide terrorist activity in the second half of the 20th century.

Century I Quatrain 20

> *Tours, Orleans, Blois, Angiers, Reims and Nantes,*
>
> *These cities disturbed by constant change,*
>
> *Tents are pitched by foreigners,*
>
> *Rivers, land and sea are shaking at Rennes.*

A forecast that the towns of the Loire valley and also at Reims would face change and the tramp of foreign armies.

This did indeed happen after the fall of Napoleon at Waterloo in 1815, after the defeat of France in the Franco-Prussian War in 1871 and again in the World Wars in the 20th century. The foreign armies were those of Germany, Britain and the USA.

Century I Quatrain 23

In the third month, at the rising of the sun,

The Boar and the Leopard meet to fight,

The tired Leopard looks to heaven

And sees an Eagle in the sun.

This is a description of the battle of Waterloo and the clash between Napolean (the Boar) and the Duke of Wellington (the Leopard).

Century I Quatrain 25

> *That which is lost is found, hidden for long centuries*
>
> *Pasteur will be hailed as a demi-god,*
>
> *When the moon achieves its great cycle,*
>
> *He will be dishonoured by other foul stories.*

Not only is Louis Pasteur named in this quatrain but the reference to the moon's great cycle points to the year 1889, the year in which the Pasteur Institute was founded.

The final line refers to attacks made on Pasteur after his death.

Century I Quatrain 26

The great one will be struck down in daylight,

The event predicted by the petition bearer,

The prediction also tells of another struck at night,

Conflict in Reims and London, pestilence in Tuscany.

This prophecy is recognized as foreseeing the assassination of the US President John F. Kennedy and also his brother Robert Kennedy.

President Kennedy was shot just after noon on 22 November 1963 in Dallas, Texas and Robert Kennedy around 1am on 5 June 1968.

The petition bearer perhaps refers to Jeane Dixon, a modern prophet who, in 1956, predicted the assasination of JFK and tried also to warn her friend Robert Kennedy.

The last line establishes the date of the Robert Kennedy assassination at the time of riots, in France and London in 1968 and 1969.

Century I Quatrain 37

A little before the setting of the sun,

Conflict has given the great people doubt:

Devasted, the seaport makes no response,

Bridge and tomb in two strange places.

A little before the setting of the sun of the Japanese Empire in 1945, the seafront and the strange places are Hiroshima and Nagasaki, both devasted by the first atomic bombs.

Century I Quatrain 46

Near Auch, Lectoure and Mirande,

A great fire will fall from the sky for 3 nights

A stupendous and marvellous event,

Soon afterwards the earth will tremble.

Could this quatrain describe the UFO sighting reported in the south west of France in 1961?

Reference may also be being made to the earthquakes hitting many parts of the world at this time.

Century I Quatrain 55

> *Under the opposite climate of Babylon*
>
> *Great will be the flow of blood*
>
> *By land, sea and air Heaven will be cruel*
>
> *There will be famine, plagues and confusion.*

At the beginning of 1991, Operation Desert Storm was unleashed against Iraq, who had invaded Kuwait in August 1990.

The allied attacks from the air, shelling from the Gulf and land invasion of Iraq in conjunction with Iraqi destruction of oilfields created great ecological damage throughout the region. Famine, illness of the civilian population in Iraq and political confusion resulted and still persists.

Century I Quatrain 63

The world is made small by less disease,

The lands will be peaceful for a long time,

Travel by air, land and sea will increase,

Then wars will begin again.

Is this a description of the period of the Cold War when the balance of nuclear power held the world in an uneasy peace?

With the collapse of the Soviet Union and the rise of nationalism worldwide, a huge number of wars of various kinds are now raging.

Century I Quatrain 60

An Emperor born close to Italy
Whose empire will be lost at great cost,
Considering the people who support him,
He is less a prince than a butcher

Napoleon Boneparte was born on the island of Corsica, which is close to Italy. His empire waxed and waned at a great cost in French lives.

Nostradamus prophecied three great Antichrist figures in history – Napoleon, Hitler and the third still in the future.

Century 1 Quatrain 67

I see a great famine approaching

Which will become universal

So long-lasting and major that people

Will pull up roots and take children from the breast.

The world is becoming more aware of the many problems which are mounting – quickly rising population, destruction of rain forests, global warming and the need for more energy amongst them.

Could these indications point to a 21st century of weather change, famines and droughts such as have not been seen for hundreds of years?

Century 1 Quatrain 70

> *In Persia, ceaseless rain, famine and war,*
>
> *A monarch betrayed by a trust too great,*
>
> *Begun and planned in France,*
>
> *A secret warning of fate.*

In 1979, the Shah of Iran was driven into exile by supporters of the fundamentalist leader Ayatollah Khomeini. Khomeini had been exiled for 14 years and in 1978 had planned and directed the uprising from Paris. The Shah had placed great trust in America and the CIA but, in the event, the USA refused to give military support of any kind.

Century 1 Quatrain 77

> *The headland juts out between two seas,*
>
> *Then there will be death by a horses bit,*
>
> *Neptune unfurls a black sail*
>
> *By Gibraltar and near Rocheval.*

In the Battle of Trafalgar the British fleet defeated the fleets of France and Spain.

The British were commanded by Lord Nelson, who died of his wounds. His flagship, *Victory* sailed home with black sails.

The defeated Admiral Villeneuve was captured and after his release was strangled by a horse's bridle on the orders of Napoleon.

Century 1 Quatrain 86

> *When the great queen is defeated*
>
> *She will show the courage of a man,*
>
> *On a horse she will pass over the river and enemy hordes,*
>
> *Followed by the sword, she will bring outrage to her faith.*

Mary Queen of Scots was eventually defeated at the Battle of Langside and escaped across the Solway Firth to seek refuge from Queen Elizabeth of England. Her lifestlye had already outraged her Catholic subjects.

Mary became the prisoner of Elizabeth and was executed in Fotheringay in 1587.

Century 1 Quatrain 90

The ring of the bell in Bordeaux and Poitiers

A great army will reach Langon

The wind from the mountain will be against the French,

When a divine omen makes itself known near Orgon

This is a prediction of an army causing alarm across the south of France.

After his escape from Elba, Napoleon landed on the south coast. It is said that an effigy of Napoleon was burned in Orgon near Salon in protest against him.

The wind against the French may refer to the poor weather in the summer of 1815, which perhaps contributed to the defeat of Napoleon at Waterloo.

Century 1 Quatrain 95

> *Twins are found in front of the monastery*
>
> *Of the heroic lineage of a monk:*
>
> *His fame through language and powerful sound,*
>
> *It will be said that the healthy survivor should be elected*

For the first time in history two popes of the same name came together, like twins. John Paul I was elected in 1978 but died less than two months later. The Polish John Paul II succeeded him and used the power of modern technology to promote his message.

Century 2

Century 2 Quatrain 1

The British make attacks in France,

With these partners there will be great advances,

Rain and cold will render the landscape uneven,

And powerful invasions will be made against Istanbul.

This prophecy envisages the dreadful conditions and battles of World War I.

It then moves on to predict the landings and unsuccessful campaign in the Dardanelle.

Century 2 Quatrain 9

The reign of the thin one will be peaceful for nine years

Then he will develop a bloody thirst,

Many people will die without faith or law,

Killed by one with a great weakness.

The power held by Adolph Hitler began with six years of peace, not nine. The remainder of the prophecy does, however, document the many many thousands of deaths caused by this evil man, the second Antichrist prophecied by Nostradamus.

Century 2 Quatrain 13

> *The body without soul will not be sacrificed,*
>
> *The day of death decided at birth,*
>
> *The soul will be made happy by the spirit*
>
> *The word seen in its eternity.*

Is this Nostradamus reflecting on life and what follows life? The eternal question will have exercised the prophet and his powers of prophecy will have focused his mind on the subject.

Century 2 Quatrain 19

> *New people come to a place without defence,*
>
> *A place previously uninhabitable,*
>
> *Meadows, houses, fields and towns to be enjoyed,*
>
> *Famine, plague and war and much land for ploughing.*

This is taken to mean the Jews who survived the Holocaust and who established the state of Israel in Palestine after World War II.

The great events in the region are encompassed in the last line.

Century 2 Quatrain 24

> *Ferocious beasts will cross rivers,*
>
> *Most of the field against Hitler,*
>
> *The leader will be drawn into a cage of iron,*
>
> *When the German child sees nothing.*

Hitler is a name which Nostradamus knew.

This quatrain tells of many nations ranged against Hitler and his allies. The rivers to the east and west of Germany failed to halt the advance of his enemies and his attempt to enthral the youth of Germany also failed.

Century 2 Quatrain 38

Many people will be condemned,
When the leaders have come together,
But one will be so damaged
That they cannot remain allies.

This is the prediction of the 1939 German-Soviet Non-Aggression Pact, which allowed Germany to strike against France and Britain with impunity. In spite of previous statements by Hitler and many intelligence reports warning of a German attack, the Soviet Union was surprised by the ruthless German invasion of June 1941.

Century 2 Quatrain 40

> *After a short interval,*
>
> *There will be a great storm by land and sea,*
>
> *The battles will be greater than before,*
>
> *Flames and creatures which will make disasters.*

This describes the years between World War I and World War II.

The terms of the Treaty of Versailles created the atmosphere of disillusionment in Germany which permitted Adolf Hitler and the Nazi party to take power and launch the Second World War.

Century 2 Quatrain 46

After a great tragedy for man a greater one comes,

The great power of the centuries moves on,

It will rain blood, milk, famine, war and plague,

Fire will be seen in the sky and a long trail of sparks.

This quatrain recognizes World War II and predicts the onset of World War III.

The weapons now available to man would produce famine and plague as well as the normal casualties of war.

Century 2 Quatrain 51

> *In London the blood of the just will be claimed,*
>
> *Burnt by lightning in twenty three the sixes,*
>
> *The old lady will lose her elevated position,*
>
> *And many of one sect will die.*

This is widely believed to be a prediction of the Great Fire of London of 1666.

The 'old lady' is an Old French term for a cathedral and probably refers to Saint Paul's.

Century 2 Quatrain 57

Before conflict the great one will fall,

The great one's death is sudden and causes great grief,

Flawed at birth, he will mostly float,

The earth is stained near the river of blood.

This is perhaps a reference to John F. Kennedy and his assassination in Dallas, the 'river of blood' meaning the Red River, is near Dallas.

He suffered certain disabilities which would explain the comment 'flawed at birth'.

Century 2 Quatrain 66

The prisoner escaped despite great dangers,

Soon there is a changed fortune for the great one.

The people are trapped in the palace,

The city is surrounded by a good augury.

Napoleon has escaped from Elba in 1815. On the way north his small band encountered the Fifth Infantry Regiment who refused to fire on him and, in fact, joined with him. The numbers in this army grew as he neared Paris where he again took power.

One hundred days later came the defeat at Waterloo, which Nostradamus considered a 'good augury'.

Century 2 Quatrain 67

The blond and the forked nose one will come to commit themselves

By the duel he will be chased out;

The exiles will revive the land

Committing the most force to the sea positions.

The blond William of Orange landed with an army in south west England in 1688. Although King James II also had an army, no battle was joined and the Glorious Revolution ended in the exile of James to France and the enthronement of William III and his Queen Mary as the first constitutional monarchs of Great Britain.

Century 2 Quatrain 74

From Sens and Autun they will come to the Rhone

To pass further towards the Pyrenees;

The people will leave the Marsh of Ancora

By land and sea great tracks will follow.

This may well be predicting the expansion of high speed trains throughout France and Italy.

Century 2 Quatrain 77

By Arcs pitch gunfire and blazes,
Screams and yelling at midnight;
Inside placed on the broken ramparts
They fled through narrow tracks

When the allied armies landed in the south of France, a detachment of American paratroopers lost their way and entered the small town of Les Arcs, inland from St Raphael. They were surprised by a superior German force and a bitter battle took place. The Americans were eventually relieved and the town was taken from the Germans.

Phosphorus mortar shells were used by the Americans, which explains the reference to pitch in the first line of the quatrain.

Century 2 Quatrain 84

> *Between Siena, Florence and Tuscany,*
>
> *Six months and nine days without rain*
>
> *A foreign language in the land of Dalmatia,*
>
> *It will spread, destroying all the land.*

This prophecy is still in the future and seems to foretell a great drought which will spread from Italy to the Balkans.

The foreign language suggests the UN personnel in Bosnia and Kosovo.

Century 2 Quatrain 90

The government of Hungary changed by life and death,

The law will be harder than domination;

Their great city howls and screams,

Castor and Pollox are enemies in contention.

The Hungarian uprising of 1956 was brutally put down by the Soviet Union. No help was forthcoming from the west as Britain, France and the USA were distracted by the Suez Crisis.

The Hungarian leader Imre Nagy and many of his supporters were shot and the country was once again under a repressive Communist government backed by the Soviet Union.

Century 2 Quatrain 95

> *The populated places will become uninhabitable,*
>
> *Great disagreement over lands;*
>
> *Government controlled by man lacking prudance,*
>
> *Then death and friction for the great brothers.*

The disagreement over lands may refer to continuing wars between Jews and Arabs. The great brothers could be Russia and the United States who came together after the Cold War, only to fall apart again as the world descends into disarray at the beginning of the 21st century.

Century 2 Quatrain 99

As interpreted by the prophet, the territory of Rome

Will be offended by the French people

But the Celtic nation will fear the hour,

The army having pushed too far to the north.

The armies of Napoleon plundered, the papal states in Italy during the campaigns of 1794 to 1798.

Nostradamus is prophecying that there will be great retribution, which will strike during the disastrous campaign in Russia.

Century 3

Century 3 Quatrain 8

> *Bordeaux, Rouen and La Rochelle together*
>
> *Will remain surrounded by the great sea,*
>
> *English, Bretons and Flemings together*
>
> *Will chase all the way to the approaches of Rouen.*

This would suggest 1944 when Britain and its allies, along with the Resistance fighters, drove the German armies out of Normandy.

Century 3 Quatrain 18

After a long rain of milk,

Several places touch the sky in Reims

Oh what a bloody battle near them,

Kings and the sons of kings will not risk approaching.

There was constant action and offences around Reims during World War I and the city was deemed too dangerous for visits from royalty.

The 'rain of milk' probably refers to the use of mustard gas.

Century 3 Quatrain 20

> *By the lands of the great river Guadalquivir*
>
> *The length of Iberia to the Kingdom of Grenada*
>
> *The Cross rejected by the Islamic people,*
>
> *A man from Cordoba will betray the land.*

In the early part of the seventeeth century the Spanish, aided by the Inquisition, began to drive the Moors from the country. The Moors were Christians, but when exiled many returned to their ancient faith of Islam.

Century 3 Quatrain 22

For six days the battle raged in front of the city,

Free after an intense and bitter struggle:

The three will surrender it and be pardoned

The remainder will have fire and bloody slaughter.

The three mentioned in this quatrain are Egypt, Syria and Jordan who were surprised by the Israeli attack in 1967– the Six Day War. The three were forced to hand Jerusalem over to Israel and slowly peace agreements were established with Egypt, Jordan and the Palestinians and possibly before long with Syria. The 'remainder' referred to may be Iran, Libya and Iraq.

Century 3 Quatrain 28

Of feeble land and poor parentage,
By blows and peace the empire is gained;
The young woman will reign long,
Never has a reign been worse.

Elizabeth I of England's mother, Anne Boleyn, was executed by her father, Henry VIII. As she grew up she was surrounded by death and fear, especially as a Protestant during the rule of Queen Mary, her stepsister. Elizabeth became Queen at the age of 25 and ruled for 45 years.

Nostradamus does not seem to rate her years in power very highly!

Century 3 Quatrain 33

In the city where the wolf will enter,

The enemy will be very close,

A great foreign country will be laid waste,

The friends will pass through frontiers and the Alps.

This appears to refer to the Second World War and the entry of Hitler the wolf, into Paris in 1940. This is followed by the arrival of the allied forces and the defeat of Germany.

Century 3 Quatrain 35

> *From deep in the west of Europe*
>
> *A child from a poor background will be born*
>
> *Who will win over vast numbers with his language,*
>
> *His fame will travel to the East.*

A prophecy about Adolf Hitler who was born in Austria of a humble background. He was a powerful demagogue who swayed the German nation in the 1930s and led Germany into the Second World War. He brought about the alliance of Germany and Japan during the war.

Century 3 Quatrain 53

When the greatest carries off the prize

Of Nuremberg, Augsburg and Basel:

Frankfurt is retaken by the leader of Cologne,

Crossing Flanders and into France.

This is another reference to Adolf Hitler, Nostradamus' second Antichrist. It foretells his political triumph in Nuremberg, the retaking of the Rhineland and the blitzbrieg through Flanders to France in 1940.

The mention of Basel perhaps acknowledges the possibility which was real, of the annexation of Switzerland into the Greater German Reich.

Century 3 Quatrain 54

> *One of the great ones will fly to Spain,*
>
> *Which will bleed from a long wound;*
>
> *Armies will pass over the high mountains,*
>
> *Great destruction and then ruling in peace.*

General Franco was exiled in the Canary Islands and later flew to mainland Spain to lead a Nationalist uprising against the Socialist government. The civil war devastated large parts of Spain and lasted from 1936 till 1939.

Once in power, Franco kept Spain out of the Second World War, in spite of his sympathies with the Nazis, who had supported him.

Century 3 Quatrain 57

> *The British people will have seven changes*
>
> *Tainted by blood for 290 years*
>
> *Not free of German influence,*
>
> *Aries uncertain of the protector of Poland.*

The seven changes in Britain are likely to be the alternating fortunes of the House of Stuart, Oliver Cromwell and the House of Hanover, the German influence. The seventh ruler was predicted as the protector of Poland, Hitler, but this part did not go according to the script.

Century 3 Quatrain 60

> *In all Asia many will be outlawed,*
>
> *Even in Mystia, Lycia and Pamphilia*
>
> *Blood will flow by absolution*
>
> *From a young black man filled with evil.*

This prophecy corners Asia, including Turkey, Iran and Iraq and seems to refer to the era of Islamic Fundamentalist terrorism which has risen in the second half of the 20th century.

Century 3 Quatrain 61

The great army and sect of all the cross

Will gather in Mesopotamia

From the nearby river will come the light company,

Whether such law will remain with the enemy.

In 1991 Operation Desert Storm was mounted against Iraq by an overwhelmingly Christian allied army.The 'light company' probably refers to airborne forces or the speed of the attack and the final line suggests that Saddam Hussein is left still holding power after the war.

Century 3 Quatrain 63

The power of Rome will be cast down,

Traces of greatness gone through imitation of its neighbour,

Secret hatred and quarrels,

Will hold back the fools and their follies.

The rise of Benito Mussolini in Italy was largely brought about by his theatrical speeches which greatly affected his listeners.

Adolf Hitler took this technique further in his mass rallies and use of uniforms and banners.

The two dictators are described here as fools or buffoons but their influence was strong and evil.

Century 3 Quatrain 65

When the tomb of a great Roman is discovered,

The next day a Pope will be elected

The Senate will not approve of him,

The sacred chalice holds his poisoned blood.

In 1978 it was claimed that the tomb of St Peter had been discovered beneath the Vatican.

Soon after that the cardinals of the Catholic Church met in conclave to elect a new Pope. Part of the election is that the cardinals place their votes in a special chalice. The new Pope, John Paul I, greatly worried the conservatives in the Church and especially the members of the Curia by his open-minded approach to modern concerns such as woman's rights and birth control. He also showed a determination to investigate the finances of the Vatican and possible connections with the underworld.

There have been many suggestions that his death was not natural and that he could have been poisoned.

Century 3 Quatrain 66

> *The great Bailiff of Orleans put to death,*
>
> *Vindicated by one of the blood:*
>
> *Not deserving the fate of death,*
>
> *Kept capture by the fleet and hands.*

During the French Revolution, Philip d'Orleans renounced his nobility and became a member of the National Assembly. In the Assembly he voted for the death of King Louis XVI, his cousin. He later fell foul of Robespierre and was executed during the Reign of Terror.

Century 3 Quatrain 68

People without a leader in Spain and Italy

Killing and death in the peninsula,

Their dictator brought down by stupidity

Blood flowing everywhere.

Spain and Italy have both been ruled by dictators in the 20th century and both countries are peninsulas.

Mussolini was killed by partisans at the end of the Second World War but Franco ruled Spain until his death in 1975.

Century 3 Quatrain 70

> *Great Britain, including England*
>
> *Will be inundated by deep waters*
>
> *The new league of Ausonia will go to war*
>
> *As they will come together against them*

Nostradamus envisages Great Britain in the future and predicts floods, which may be caused by global warming.

The quatrain also seems to indicate a time when there will be great terrorist activity in Italy.

Century 3 Quatrain 71

> *Those in the islands will be under siege for a long time,*
>
> *They will take strong action against their enemies;*
>
> *Those outside die of hunger,*
>
> *Greater starvation has never been known.*

After the fall of France in the Second World War, Britain stood alone against the all-conquering German forces and suffered greatly from bombing attacks and attempts to cut off supplies coming to the islands by sea. During 1941 the RAF stepped up night bombing raids on German cities and areas of production.

The people of Europe outside of Great Britain were suffering terrible hunger in addition to the millions of deaths in occupied countries and concentration camps.

Century 3 Quatrain 75

> *Pau, Verona, Vicenza, Saragossa*
>
> *Bloody swords from distant lands.*
>
> *A great plague will arrive with scabs,*
>
> *Help is close but the remedies will take time.*

This could well be a prophecy of the AIDS virus sweeping through France, Italy and Spain from Africa. Much of the work on the new disease is carried out at the Institute Pasteur in France.

Century 3 Quatrain 82

Frejus, Antibes, towns around Nice,

Will be greatly damaged by land and sea

The wind fair on both land and sea,

There will be death, capture and pillage outwith the laws of war.

The Americans landed in the south of France in the Gulf of Frejus and fought along the coast past Nice. Much of the property where the troops landed was severely damaged.

Century 3 Quatrain 84

> *The grand city will always be devastated,*
>
> *No inhabitants will remain,*
>
> *Buildings, temples and women violation*
>
> *People will die by guns, fire and plague.*

This would appear to signal the total devastation of Berlin by the Russians in 1945. The destruction of the city was complete and the civilian population suffered death, homelessness and widespread rape.

Century 3 Quatrain 94

For another five hundred years they will value him,

He who was the light of his time,

Then there will be a great revelation,

Which will please exceedingly the people of that century.

This is a difficult prophecy which seems to suggest that the true meanings of the prophecies of Nostradamus will not become known until 500 years after their publication. This would point to the year 2055.

Century 3 Quatrain 97

> *There will be a new law and a new land,*
>
> *Around Syria, Jordan and Palestine*
>
> *The great Barbarian empire will perish,*
>
> *Before the end of the Century of the Sun.*

This indicates that a lasting peace will be established between Israel and the surrounding Arab states. The time for this great breakthrough is at the end of the 20th century, the Century of the Sun.

Century 3 Quatrain 99

In the grassy fields of Alleins and Vernegues,

With the mountains of the Luberon near the Durance,

The conflict will be bitter in the two areas,

Mesopotamia will not succeed in France.

Nostradamus is seeing future battles to be fought around his home town of Salon.

In 1944 there was fierce fighting around the river Durance between the retreating German army and the Americans advancing from the south coast, supported by the Resistance.

The Paris region is sometimes referred to as Mesopotamia in France because of the similar river system of the Marne and the Seine.

The last line of the quatrain may be describing the German occupation of Paris between 1940 and 1944.

Century 4

Century 4 Quatrain 2

> *Because of death, France will journey to action,*
>
> *The fleet by sea and the army marching over the Pyrenees,*
>
> *Spain in trouble, soldiers on the march,*
>
> *Some of the greatest Ladies taken to France.*

This prophecies the War of the Spanish Succession (1701-1714). The marriages of the daughters of Philip III and Philip IV of Spain into the French royal line caused the war when Charles II of Spain declared that his succesor would be his cousin, Louis XIV of France.

The war pitted France against Austria, Britain, Holland, Prussia and Savoy.

Century 4 Quatrain 5

Cross, peace carried out by one with the divine word,

Spain and France will be joined:

Great disaster is approaching and combat bitter,

The heart so hard that it cannot be moved.

Napoleon invaded Spain in1808 and annexed it to France. There was fierce guerilla warfare for many years and France lost huge numbers of men. It is notable that Napoleon never returned to Spain to take command of his army there.

Century 4 Quatrain 11

> *The one who will govern in the great cape,*
>
> *Will be led to move in some cases:*
>
> *The twelve reds will come to search the cover,*
>
> *Murder will be carried out.*

This is another prophecy about the death of Pope John Paul I in 1978.

He is the one in the 'great cape' and was determined to change the hierarchy in the Vatican. 'The twelve reds' are the cardinals in the Curia and there have been accusations that they arranged to get rid of the Pope before he had the opportunity to investigate the background to his suspicions too deeply.

Century 4 Quatrain 12

The greatest army put to flight on the road

It will hardly be chased further :

The expeditions force regrouped and the legion reduced,

Then they will all be chased out of France.

In 1940 it was believed that France had the most powerful army in Europe and was more than a match for the German army. The Blitzkreigh showed this belief to be wrong and soon the Frnech were put to flight and the British Expeditionary Force made its famous escape from Dunkirk.

Over the next few years the British army regrouped and in 1944 landed in Normandy with the Americans and chased the Germans out of France.

Century 4 Quatrain 23

> *The legion in the naval fleet,*
>
> *Lime, magnesium, sulphur and pitch will burn*
>
> *A long time as safe places*
>
> *Genoa and Monaco will be consumed by fire.*

The invasion of the south of France was mainly carried out by American troops, supported by Free French divisions.

The second line would appear to be an attempted description of flame throwers. Until 1944 Provence had been a fairly quiet part of Vichy controlled France but with the invasion, the fighting extended from Monaco to Marseilles and then inland.

Century 4 Quatrain 25

Sublime bodies without end visible to the eye,

They come to obsess the mind for their own reasons

Body and brow, main senses invisible

The sacred prayers die away.

This would appear not to be a prophecy but a description of Nostradamus preparing himself through meditation. He settled himself at night in his secret study and, with the help of the stars and his own meditation contemplated the future direction of the world.

Century 4 Quatrain 27

> *Salon, Mausol, Tarascon from the Sex Arch,*
>
> *Where still the pyramid stands:*
>
> *They will come to surrender the Prince Dannemarc,*
>
> *Redemption honoured at the temple of Artemis*

Nostradamus appears to be reflecting on the area of his birth.Mausole is a priory just outside St Remy. It latterly became an insane asylum and it was here that Van Gogh was held shortly before his suicide in 1890.

The reference to the Sex Arch is not what it seems! Beside the priory is a Roman arch with an inscription which reads: SEX.L.M.JUIEI, the name of the Roman honoured by the arch.

The last two lines of the quatrain are very obscure and have not been adequately interpreted.

Century 4 Quatrain 28

> *When Venus is covered by the Sun,*
>
> *A secret form will be under the splendour:*
>
> *Mercury will uncover them to the fire,*
>
> *By the noise of battle it will be insulted.*

Venus is hidden twice a year when it comes into conjunction with the Sun. Such a conjunction will take place on 9 June 2000 and at the same time Mercury will be seen in the sky just before dawn. The suggestion is that an act of war or terrorism will take place then.

Century 4 Quatrain 31

> *The Moon in the middle of the night on the high mountain,*
>
> *The young wise man has seen it in his mind:*
>
> *Through his disciples he will be immortal*
>
> *His eyes to the south, hands on breast, body to the fire.*

Again the prophet is describing his nocturnal contemptions and he is sensing that the ideas and beliefs will live on after his death, through his disciples.

Century 4 Quatrain 32

The time will come for flesh to give way to fish,

The law of the people will be changed:

The old ways will remain, although not always seen,

And communism will be strongly pushed back.

A prophecy of the end of communism. The old ways of the people survived the years of domination and the ideas which erupted at the time of the Russian revolution were rejected much sooner than anyone could have predicted.

Century 4 Quatrain 35

> *The fire will die, the virgins will betray*
>
> *The greatest part of the new band:*
>
> *An iron thunderbolt and a lance will guard the only king,*
>
> *Tuscany and Corsica, throats cut by night.*

In ancient Rome the vestal virgins guarded the eternal flame of the goddess of the hearth. This is a prediction that Italy will betray the old values and turn to the fascists of Mussolini. The Axis forces left Corsica in 1943 and Tuscany experienced bitter fighting towards the end of the war in Italy.

Century 4 Quatrain 36

New sports take place in France

After the victory in Lombardy:

In the western mountains the great ones are bound:

Romania and Spain shake with fear.

Napoleon had a successful campaign in northern Italy during 1798 and also at this time there was a renewal of interest in all forms of athletics and sport. Ten years later Napoleon invaded Spain and took the Spanish king prisoner.

Century 4 Quatrain 40

> *The fortresses of the besieged are condemned*
>
> *By explosives in deep places:*
>
> *The betrayers will be buried alive,*
>
> *A pitiful separation of the Saxons.*

At the end of the Second World War in April 1945, Hitler was besieged in his fortified bunker in Berlin. It was here, deep underground, that he took his own life.

The final line of the quatrain probably refers to the division of Germany, which lasted until 1990.

Century 4 Quatrain 48

The vast fertile plains of Italy

Will produce so many locusts

That the light from the sun will be clouded,

They will devour everything and bring a great plague.

There have been warnings that the plagues of locusts which denude large parts of Africa could reach Italy and the south of France. The changes taking place now in climate could well bring about such a change.

Century 4 Quatrain 51

> *A duke keen to trace his enemy,*
>
> *Will enter by stopping the phalanx*
>
> *Rushing on foot and following closely,*
>
> *On the day of battle near the Ganges.*

In 1764 was fought the battle of Buxar, in India, near the river Ganges. A small British army, with native troops, defeated a much larger army of the Nawab of Bengal. As a result, Britain gained Oude and other territories in India. During the battle the British held their ground against the larger force and then charged and routed them.

Century 4 Quatrain 54

A name never given to the Gallic King,

Never was there a more terrible thunderbolt:

Italy, Spain and English are shaken,

Greatly attentive to women from abroad.

This quatrain again speaks of Napoleon Bonaparte who never became King, but assumed the title of Emperor.

His armies shook the whole of Europe and completely altered the bace of the continent. The women in his life were from outside France. His first wife and Empress, Josephine, came from Haiti, the opera singer Guiseppina Grassini was Italian and the countess Maria Walewska was Polish.

Century 4 Quatrain 56

> *After the victory of the raving tongue,*
>
> *The spirit becomes tranquil and at rest:*
>
> *The bloody victor lectures through the war,*
>
> *Burning the tongue, flesh and bones.*

Hitler's greatest weapon in his rise to power was his electrifying speeches. He could raise his audiences to fever pitch and he incited his nation with regular speeches during the first half of the war. It was said that he was both physically and mentally exhausted after each speech.

After his suicide in Berlin his body was burned, as forecast in the fourth line.

Century 4 Quatrain 61

The old man is mocked and robbed of his position,

By the foreigner who will bribe him:

His son's hands consumed before his face,

The brother betrayed at Chartres, Orleans and Rouen.

The prophet is describing the situation in France almost 400 years after his death.

The country was occupied by Germany and much of it was ruled by the puppet Vichy government headed by France's hero of the First World War. Marshal Petain, whose nickname was 'the old man'. The powers of France had been taken away and in August 1944 Petain was sent to prison in Germany. At the same time the Allied armies were liberating Chartres, Orleans and Rouen.

Century 4 Quatrain 62

> *A colonel will mount an ambitious plot,*
>
> *He will seize most of the army.*
>
> *In a secret coup against his Prince,*
>
> *And he will be uncovered under his leafy boughs.*

It is not entirely clear who the colonel could be, but the details seem to point to Colonel Gaddafih of Libya.

In 1969 he mounted a secret coup and overthrew the government of King Idrish. Libya has gained a reputation as a refuge for Islamic terrorists and has undoubtably been responsible for many attacks against the West.

The final line of the quatrain may point to Gaddafi's regular lifestyle of living in a Bedouin tent on the edge of the desert.

Century 4 Quatrain 68

In the year close to Venus

The two greatest of Asia and Africa,

From the Rhine and Hitler is said to arrive

Cries and tears in Malta and the coast of Liguria

The year of Venus is reckoned to be 1939 and the 'two greatest' referred to would be Japan and Italy,with her African colonies.

This is also a prophecy of the long and violent siege of Malta.

Century 4 Quatrain 71

> *In place of a wedding the girls were killed,*
>
> *A murder of great evil, with no survivors*
>
> *Inside the virgins were drowned*
>
> *And the bride poisoned.*

This could well relate to the execution in 1918 of the Russian Czar and all his family in Ekaterinberg. The bodies were thrown down a flooded mine shaft. There have been many theories regarding the execution and the possible escape of one of the Czar's daughters, Anastasia.

Century 4 Quatrain 80

Near the great river a great ditch created,

The water. divided into 15 parts;

The city captured, fire, blood, cries and battle,

And most concerned with the collision.

This quatrain foretells the building of the Maginot Line in eastern France as a defence against further German invasions after the First World War. The French believed that these defences provided total safety but in 1940, the German armoured attack smashed through Holland and Belgium, outflanking the Maginot Line and leaving northern France and Paris exposed.

Century 4 Quatrain 89

> *Thirty men from London will plot in secret*
>
> *Against their king on the sea invasion,*
>
> *The king's party disgusted by death,*
>
> *A fair haired king from Friesland elected .*

This is a very exact prophecy of the conspiracy against James II and the crowning of William of Orange as king and co-ruler of England.

Twenty-nine lords in London signed the request to William to lead what became the Glorious Revolution, so called because of a lack of bloodshed. James feared the same end as his grandfather , Charles I and fled to France leaving the fair haired William from Friesland as king in his place.

Century 4 Quatrain 93

A serpent seen close to the royal bed,

The lady's dogs will not bark by night:

Then will be born in France a very royal Prince.

Sent from heaven for all Princes to see.

This quatrain appears to set out to please Queen Catherine de Medici, the patron and great friend of Nostradamus. Catherine had a serpent in her coat of arms and it was said that the dogs which guarded her bedchamber did not bark when she was visited by her husband, the future Henry II of France. Nostradamus then praises the birth of her first born.

Century 4 Quatrain 96

The elder sister of the British Isles
Will exist 15 years before her brother;
By the promise he has kept,
She will achieve balanced rule.

Britain's elder sister represents the American Colonies which won their independence 15 years before the French Revolution. The Americans were aided in their struggle by the French and both countries established republics and democratic rule.

Century 5

Century 5 Quatrain 4

> *The great Bulldog expelled from the city*
>
> *Will be made angry by the foreign pact;*
>
> *After the stag was hunted to fields,*
>
> *The wolf and the bear will clash.*

Normally when 'the city' is referred to it is assumed to be Paris. This would seem to predict Winston Churchill's attempt to convince the French government to continue the fight against Germany in 1940 and his anger at the pact between Vichy France and Germany. Lines three and four follow the war to the east and describe the struggle between Hitler (the wolf) and Russia (the bear).

Century 5 Quatrain 7

The bones of the Triumoir will be found

After deep searching for an obscure treasure

Those nearby will not be at rest :

This marble and lead coffin.

Napoleon had been a member of a Triumoirate ruling France and in 1840 his body was brought back from St Helena for burial at the Hotel des Invalides in Paris.

Century 5 Quatrain 21

> *By the demise of the Latin King*
>
> *By those he helped during his reign:*
>
> *The fire will glow, he body divided*
>
> *The public death of the brazen ones.*

This foretells the death of Mussolini. Having led Italy for many years, giving the people promises of glory and booty, in 1945 he was killed by his own people. His body and that of his mistress were hung by their feet in public and reviled by the mob.

Century 5 Quatrain 26

> *The Slav people through good fortune in war*
>
> *Will be raised very high:*
>
> *They will change their prince to one born as a provincial,*
>
> *Raised in the mountains to cross the sea.*

Soviet people will repulse the German armies which invaded their country. The last line predicts the Soviet army in the Caucasius being transported across the Black Sea to recapture the Crimea.The change of prince would appear to see the death of Stalin a few years after the end of the war and the emergence of Nikita Kruschev as leader.

Century 5 Quatrain 32

> *Where everything is good and well in Sun and Moon*
>
> *And plentiful, its ruin draws near:*
>
> *The winnowing of your fortune comes from the sky,*
>
> *In the same state as the seventh rock.*

This is a prophecy of disaster following good times. It could be the result of a nuclear war or perhaps a natural diaster brought about by global warming, leading to rising oceans, hurricanes and droughts. Some interpreters have forecast this catastrophe for the 2030s.

Century 5 Quatrain 38

The one who will succeed this great monarch,

Will live an illicit and lecherous life,

Through carelessness he will give away away everything.

Ending in the failure of Salic Law.

King Louis XIV of France was known as the Great Monarch.

This quatrain tells of his great-grandson who became Louis XV and who lived a life of hedonism. He was renowned for his appetites for food, drink and women and allowed one of his mistresses, Madame de Pompadour, to run the affairs of state. This broke the Salic law which excluded women from succession to the throne.

His successor Louis XVI paid the price of the poverty and anger of the people.

Century 5 Quatrain 41

Born under the shadows and on a day as night,

He will reign in goodness:

His blood will be reborn in the ancient urn,

Replacing the century of gold for brass.

Is a new world or spiritual leader to emerge having been born during a total eclipse of the sun?

The mountain of the ancient urn indicates Aquarius the Water-Bearer and the Age of Aquarius has been forecast for early in the 21st century.

Century 5 Quatrain 56

> *Following the death of the very old Pope,*
>
> *A Roman of good age will be elected:*
>
> *It will be said that he weakened the Holy See*
>
> *And for a long time was involved in intrigue.*

Pope Paul VI was elected on the death of the old and very popular Pope John XXIII. Paul was a clever man who travelled extensively but it was claimed that he weakened the position of the Holy See by his involvement in some suspect financial dealings of the Vatican Bank.

Century 5 Quatrain 63

> *From the vain use of honour and undeserved complaint,*
>
> *The wandering vessel near the Latin suffering cold and hunger:*
>
> *The land is bloodstained near the Tiber,*
>
> *And mankind will have several plagues.*

Several interpreters of Nostradamus detect, in some of his quatrains, references to terrorists in our time.

This prophecy seems to concern terrorists off the Italian coast in a small vessel, perhaps a submarine. The plagues mentioned could be the result of a nuclear attack.

Century 5 Quatrain 74

There will be born of Trojan blood and German heart,

One who will become so powerful:

He will banish the foreign Arabic people,

Returning the Church to its former high position.

It was said that the French royalty was decended from the Trojans.

This prediction could see Jean-Marie Le Pen, the right wing neo-nazi leader of the National Front in France coming to power and driving out the North African emigrants who have settled in France in recent times.

Century 5 Quatrain 78

> *The two will not be united for long,*
>
> *And in thirteen years the power of Barbary:*
>
> *The two sides will suffer such loss,*
>
> *That the Bark and cape will be blessed*

The two referred to in the first line could be Russia and the United States, whose détente could be upset by North African terrorist activity.

Nostradamus could also be pointing to the end of the world.

Century 5 Quatrain 81

> *The royal bird over the city of the sun,*
>
> *Seven months in advance it will make a prophecy by night:*
>
> *The wall in the east will come down with thunder and lightening*
>
> *The enemy by now at the gates in seven days.*

When applied to the situation in France in 1940 this is a remarkable prophecy. The city of the sun is Paris and in the autumn of 1939 German planes dropped leaflets over Northern France containing Nostradamus' prophecies of the fall of France in order to affect the morale of the population.

This was seven months before the German assault which outflanked the Maginot Line by striking through Holland and Belgium and surprising the French and British armies. The final push to Paris took seven days.

Century 5 Quatrain 85

> *In Switzerland and surrounding areas*
>
> *There will be a war caused by the clouds:*
>
> *Swarms of locusts and insects,*
>
> *The faults of Geneva will be well shown.*

This quatrain speaks of a catastrophe caused by the clouds, which may well point to the crisis which is now exercising the world community regarding pollution and the greenhouse effect.

The mention of Switzerland suggests that the agencies of the United Nations in Geneva have failed to handle the situation and wars may break out caused by panic.

Century 5 Quatrain 90

> *In the Cyclades, Perinthus and Larissa,*
>
> *Inside Sparta and the Peloponnese:*
>
> *So great a famine and pestilence by error,*
>
> *It will remain for nine months in all the peninsula.*

Nostradamus often prophecied disasters which could be nuclear accidents, or even terrorist attacks in Italy or the Balkans. If either of these events occur, the nuclear fallout would undoubtedly affect the whole of Greece and the surrounding area.

At the present time there is great concern over the state of nuclear power stations in Eastern Europe and the Balkans.

Century 5 Quatrain 91

> *At the great market there is talk of deceit,*
>
> *Of all the torrenth and the field of Athens:*
>
> *There will be surprise at the light horsemen*
>
> *Of Albania, Mars, Leo and Saturn in conjunction.*

The great market is the European Union and the dating in the last line points to the year 1993.

The quatrain predicts the turmoil of the Balkans and beyond, with the feared involvement of Greece, brought about by the bitter wars fought in Bosnia and Kosovo.

Century 5 Quatrain 93

> *Under the land of the round globe of the moon,*
>
> *When Mercuy will be dominant:*
>
> *The Scottish Isles will bring forth a learned person,*
>
> *Who will discomfi the English.*

The domination of Mercury could point to the period before 2008 and this predicition perhaps refers to Charles, Prince of Wales. He has always been most comfortable in the relative tranquillity of Scotland,which explains the mention of that country . He will step forward to be crowned King Charles III before the year 2008.

Century 5 Quatrain 94

> *He will incorporate into a Greater Germany*
>
> *Brabant and Flanders, Ghent, Bruges and Bologna:*
>
> *The false treaty, the great Duke of Armenia*
>
> *Will attack Vienna and Cologne.*

Nostradamus returns to one of his recurring subjects – Hitler and the rise and fall of Nazi Germany.

Some of Hitler's early conquests are listed and then there is reference to the 'false treaty' This was the Non-Aggression Pact which was signed in 1939 by Germany and the Soviet Union. In 1941 Hitler broke the pact by invading the Soviet Union but did not have the spectacular victory which he planned.

The Duke of Armenia is Stalin, who was born in Georgia and knew Armenia well.

The last line refers to the stunning victory which Stalin eventually accomplished.

Century 5 Quatrain 97

The deformed one suffocated by horror,

In the city lived in by the Great King:

The strict edict of the captives is revoked,

Hail and thunder incalculable in Condom.

A legend grew of the man in the Iron Mask, who was thought to be the deformed twin brother of Louis XIV of France. He spent most of his life imprisoned and his identity was concealed by an iron mask.

The city is Paris and it was there in 1685 that Louis XIV revoked the Edict of Nantes, thus taking away the Hugenots' freedom of worship which was established by the edict.

Century 5 Quatrain 99

> *Milan, Ferrara, Turin and Aquileia,*
>
> *Capua, Brindisi upset by the Celtic people:*
>
> *By the Lion and the ranks of the eagle*
>
> *When Rome will have the old British chief.*

There have been various interpretations of this prophecy but the one which makes most sense is that it describes the advance of the British and American armies in Italy in 1944 and 1945. The 'old British chief' in that case would be Winston Churchill.

Century 6 Quatrain 2

> *In the year five hundred and eighty, more or less,*
>
> *A very strange century is awaited:*
>
> *In the year seven hundred and three the heavens can testify,*
>
> *That several kingdoms will change, one to five.*

This is an unusual quatrain as exact dates are predicted. 1580 saw the beginning of the Seventh War of Religion in France and in 1703 the War of the Spanish Succession began. Louis XIV's grandson became Philip V of Spain and Milan, the Netherlands and the Two Sicilies were integrated into the Spanish Empire.

At the end of this war, the Treaty of Utrecht effectively ended Louis XIV's attempts to expand in Europe.

Century 6 Quatrain 3

The river which tests the Celtic newly born,

Will be in great dispute with the Empire:

Because of the men of the church, the young prince

Will take the crowned sceptre of harmony.

In early days the French would test a newborn king by forcing him to swim in the river Rhine. The possible king referred to in this quatrain is likely to be either Louis XIII or his son Louis XIV. Both were advised by cardinals, Louis XIII by Richelieu and Louis XIV by Magarin. Both Cardinals urged their king towards war and many of the battles took place along the Rhine.

Century 6 Quatrain 9

> *There will be scandals at the sacred temples,*
>
> *Which will be considered as honourable,*
>
> *By one engraved on silver and gold medals,*
>
> *The end will be in torment very strange.*

This could be another allusion to the scandals over the Vatican Bank and the events surrounding the death of Pope John Paul I.

The man deeply involved was Bishop Paul Marcinkus, who was confined to Vatican City because of the threat of police action against him in Italy.

Century 6 Quatrain 10

In a little time the temple of colours

Black and white will intermingle.

The reds and yellows will take what is theirs,

Blood, earth, plague, hunger, fire, thirst.

This would appear to be a look ahead to our times or beyond. The mixing of faiths and races are envisaged and also various catastrophes which will be inflicted on the world. Global warming, AIDS, lack of water and famine are all disasters which are waiting to happen perhaps in the not too distant future.

Century 6 Quatrain 13

> *One who is doubtful will not come far to reign,*
>
> *The majority will wish to support him:*
>
> *A Capitol will not want him to reign,*
>
> *He will not be able to bear his great tribulation.*

This is a clear prophecy of the rise and great fall of Richard Nixon as President of the United States. There was always a doubt in many minds of how honest Nixon was. He was however, able to reach the silent majority in the 1968 presidential election and became president in January 1969.

When the details of the Watergate scandal emerged in 1974 the Democrat controlled congress in the Capitol voted for his impeachment and forced his resignation.

Century 6 Quatrain 19

The true flame will overwhelm the lady,

Who will want to put the Innocents to the fire:

Close to the assault there will be excitement,

When a beef monster will be seen in Seville.

This foresees developments in the Wars of Religion in France when the Queen, Catherine de Medici, exhausts her patience with the tolerance being shown to the Huguenots. This led to the St Bartholemew's Day Massacre of many Hugernots in 1572.

Century 6 Quatrain 26

> *The seat will be taken for four years,*
>
> *The one who will take it knows the world:*
>
> *Ravenna, Pisa and Verona will give support,*
>
> *Wishing to raise the cross of the Pope.*

Pope John XXIII reigned for four and a half years until June 1963. He brought great changes to the Papacy and was much loved for his knowledge of the world, cleverness and good humour. He was a man who loved people and he changed the Catholic Church forever.

Century 6 Quatrain 33

His final power is by bloody Alus,

He will not be able to guard himself by sea:

Between two rivers fearing military force,

The black one will bring the angry one to repentance.

Saddam Hussein is the angry one who lives between the Tigris and the Euphrates rivers. He is vulnerable to attack from the sea and he expects further military threats from the West. The black one could perhaps be an Iranian leader who has still to emerge.

Century 6 Quatrain 35

> *Near the Great Bear and close to the Milky Way,*
>
> *Aries, Taurus, Cancer, Leo, Virgo*
>
> *Mars, Jupiter, the Sun will scorch the great plain,*
>
> *Woods and cities, letters hidden by the candle.*

Mars, Jupiter and the Sun passed through the above constellations a few times in recent years. During one of these periods, in summer 1987, Provence and the French Riviera experienced ravaging drought and forest fires.

The same three planets will come together again in 2011 and a serious drought could be expected that year.

Century 6 Quatrain 37

> *The former work will perfect itself,*
>
> *Great evil will fall on the great one from the roof:*
>
> *An innocent will be accused of the death:*
>
> *The one who is guilty concealed in bushes and mist.*

If this prophecy is applied to the assassination of President Kennedy in 1963, it is remarkably clear and damning. It was the conclusion of the Warren Commission, which investigated the killing, that the president was shot by one man, Lee Harvey Oswald, from a top window in the Texas School Book Depository in Dallas.

Oswald claimed he had been used as a patsy and many witnesses stated that shots had been fired from the Grassy Knoll, which was from a different direction.

Could an innocent man have been accused and paid with his life and could the guilty man, hidden in the bushes, have been spirited away to safety?

Century 6 Quatrain 49

> *The great Pontiff of the party of war*
>
> *Will gain control of the borders of the Danube:*
>
> *To chase the cross by the crooked cross,*
>
> *Captives, gold, rings, more than one hundred thousand rubies.*

Hitler was born and brought up near the banks of the Danube in Austria. This quatrain foresees his eventual domination of Austria, Czechoslovakia, Hungary and Romania.

The crooked cross is the swastika, the emblem of the Nazi Party and Nostradamus sees the aquiescence of the Catholic Church in Rome to the expansion of Nazi Rule in Europe.

The last line describes the millions of captives and the plundered riches of the defeated countries.

Century 6 Quatrain 51

The people assembled to see a new sight,

Princes and Kings in the large audience:

Pillars and walls collapse but like a miracle

The King is saved and thirty others.

On 8th November 1939 Hitler made his annual speech at the Munich Beer Hall. The hall was full and many senior Nazis were present. For some reason which was never fully explained, Hitler left the rally early. Minutes after his departure a bomb exploded, killing seven and injuring many others.

Century 6 Quatrain 63

> *The lone lady living in the realm*
>
> *Her first husband dead on a bed of honour:*
>
> *She will weep with sadness for seven years,*
>
> *Then long life for the kingdom and good fortune.*

Catherine de Medici mourned the death of her husband, King Henry II, for seven years.

During her long life she acted as regent for her sons Francis II and Charles IX and contributed greatly to the stability of the Kingdom of France.

Century 6 Quatrain 72

> *By the fury of divine emotion,*
>
> *The wife of the great man strongly violated:*
>
> *The judges wish to damn such a creed,*
>
> *The victim sacrificed to the ignorant people.*

This refers to the situation in Russia just before the revolution. Rasputin, the monk and healer, gained great influence over the Czarina when he healed her son, the Czarovitch, and it was rumoured that he seduced her. A group of aristocrats eventually succeeded in killing Rasputin.

The last line forecasts the execution of the Czar, Czarina and their family by the Bolsheviks.

Century 6 Quatrain 74

> *The woman driven from power will return,*
>
> *Her enemies among schemers:*
>
> *She will, however triumph in time,*
>
> *Three and seventy, assured until death.*

Napoleon III's Empress Eugenie advised him in many things and she had many enemies at court. When the emperor was deposed by the National Assembly, Eugenie went into exile with him in England. The Emperor died in 1873 (three and seventy) but Eugenie lived a full life and died in 1920.

Century 6 Quatrain 80

> *From Fez the reign will reach out to the peoples of Europe,*
>
> *Their city in flames, the sword will wound:*
>
> *The great one of Asia a large army by land and sea,*
>
> *Causing the blues, Persians and the cross to be driven to death.*

This is a recurring theme in the prophecies of Nostradamus. He sees the coming of a powerful ruler in China who forms an alliance with the Islamic nations to combat the supremacy of Russia and the West.

The dating of this supposed Third World War is before 2020.

Century 6 Quatrain 84

> *The one who could not rule in Sparta because of his lameness,*
>
> *He will accomplish much by seductive means:*
>
> *He will eventually be accused*
>
> *Of having a different view from the King.*

There have been many guesses about the identity of the lame man who disagreed with this leader. It could possibly be Josef Goebbels, the Nazi minister of Propaganda. It was known that he held diferent views from Hitler at times on how to project the Nazi message.

Century 6 Quatrain 88

A great kingdom will be miserable,

They will come together near the Ebro:

The mountains of the Pyrenees will bring consolation,

While in May the earth will tremble.

The Civil War in Spain seems to fit this quatrain well.

The fighting at the Ebro, the refugees crossing the Pyrenees into France and all of this taking place at the outbreak of the Second World War with catastrophe about to hit France.

Century 6 Quatrain 92

> *Prince of beauty and grace,*
>
> *The leader made second by treachery:*
>
> *The city of the blade, the face destroyed*
>
> *By a heinous murder, the head of the hated king.*

The prince of beauty would appear to be Louis XVI of France who was brought low by the revolution. After his execution by guillotine, the executioner held up his severed head for the mob to see.

Century 6 Quatrain 97

> *The sky will be in flames at 45 degrees*
>
> *Fire comes from the great new city,*
>
> *A huge flame will immediately flare,*
>
> *When it is wished that the Normans make sure.*

Could this refer to something which happened as close as 1999?

Belgrade , the capital of Serbia was bombed by NATO forces during the Kosovo crisis and it is located very close to latitude 45. The reference to the Normans could indicate NATO.

Century 6 Quatrain 99

The educated enemy will turn around in confusion,

The great army powerless and beaten by ambushes,

He will be refused the Pyrenees and Pennines,

Antique vessels found near the river.

Napoleon was a well educated man and this quatrain would indicate the beginning of the break up of his empire. In Spain he had to fight a difficult war and was eventually defeated and, at the same time, all other paths were being denied to him.

Century 6 Quatrain 100

Incantation of the Law Against Inept critics

Those reading this verse should study it deeply,

The propane and vulgar should not approach:

Also all Astrologers, Fools and Barbarians,

Who does otherwise will be subject to the sacred rite.

At the end of Century 6, Nostradamus issues a warning to the army of people through the ages who will debunk his prophecies or use them for their own ends.

He seems to have been confident that his lines would be studied and argued about long after his death.

Century 7

Century 7 Quatrain 1

> *The arch of the treasurer by Achilles cut down,*
>
> *From writings, the quadrangle made known:*
>
> *The royal action will make the comment known,*
>
> *The body will be hung in the sight of the people.*

In 1617 the Chief Minister of France, Concino Concini, was exposed and accused of fraud and corruption. Although a favourite of the Queen Regent, the 16 year-old King Louis XIII gave orders for the killing of Concini. He was shot by members of the king's guard and his body was hung up for all to see.

Century 7 Quatrain 3

After the French naval victory,

Those from Barcelona, Salon and Marseilles,

Gold stolen, the anvil inside the ball,

Those of Ptolon will take the part in the deception.

The Allied invasion of southern France in 1944 was called Operation Anvil. Although the mention of Barcelona is not correct, fighting did take place around Salon and there was a major battle for Marseilles.

Century 7 Quatrain 6

> *Naples, Palermo and all of Sicily,*
>
> *Will be left uninhabited by the hand of the barbarians*
>
> *Corsica, Salerno and the island of Sardinia,*
>
> *Hunger, plague, the end of war from greater evil.*

This is a quatrain dealing with a dreadful sequence of hunger, plague and war, in time leading to a new era of peace.

The Mediterranean is the focus of action, which could be a conventional war or a nuclear disaster affecting this area.

Century 7 Quatrain 8

Florence flee, flee the approaching Roman,

Battle will be joined at Fiesole:

Bloodshed, the great ones captured,

Neither temple nor sex will be pardoned.

This is an unfulfilled prophecy and one which is unlikely to happen. Fiesole is perched in the hills above Florence, affording a view over the Arno valley. Even Nostradamus can get things wrong!

Century 7 Quatrain 11

> *The royal child will hate his mother,*
>
> *Eye, wounded feet, rude, disobedient,*
>
> *News for the lady, strange and bitter,*
>
> *More than five hundred of her supporters will be killed.*

This is another reference to the assasination of Concini, Chief Minister of France, also covered in Quatrain of Century 7. The very young Louis XIII hated his mother, Marie de Medici, and ordered the killing of her favourite , Concimo Concini, who had colluded with Marie in fraud and corruption. It was said that over 500 supporters of Marie de Medici were killed during what was in fact, a coup.

Century7 Quatrain 19

The fort of Nice will not be attacked,
It will be defeated by bright metal,
What happens will be long discussed,
Strange and dreadful to the people.

There was a reported sighting of a UFO near Nice in 1954. Apparently the object was oval shaped and appeared to be made of aluminium. This was seen by a few witnesses and perhaps also by Nostradamus.

Century 7 Quatrain 22

The citizens of Mesopotamia

Angry against their friends,

Games, rites, feasts and everyone sleeping,

Vicar of Rome, the city captured and those of Ausonia.

This suggests that the people of Iraq are angry against the Russians, after the Gulf War of 1991. The Russian people appear to be returning to the easier paths of Communism, rather than the hard road of democracy.

The last line is forecasting the time of the last pope in Rome, perhaps in the 21st century.

Century 7 Quatrain 32

One will be born and climb the Royal mountain

Who will take over finances

To raise troops for the march on Milan,

And draw from Florence gold and men.

Mussolini was of humble birth, but after the rise of his fascist party, he was invited by the King of Italy to form a Government.

He controlled Italy for 15 years or more before the Second World War, but in time his disastrous military decisions brought about the complete collapse of his country and the deaths of many, many thousands of Italians.

Century 7 Quatrain 33

> *By fraud, the kingdom's forces stripped,*
> *The fleet blockaded and watched:*
> *Two false friends will rally,*
> *To renew a long hidden hatred.*

This could well describe the dramatic events after the capitulation of France in 1940.

The French fleet was in harbour at the fort of Mers-el-Kebir in Algeria and Churchill decided that this large fleet of almost 20 warships should surrender to their former allies, the British, or be destroyed. The French Admiral refused to join the Royal Navy and almost all the ships were sunk or badly damaged, with the loss of almost 1300 lives.

The French anger and hatred was very great.

Century 7 Quatrain 34

> *The people of Gaul will have great regret,*
>
> *With a vain heart, they believe in rashness,*
>
> *Bread, salt, no wine, water: poison, no ale,*
>
> *Great imprisonment, hunger, cold and wont.*

Another quatrain covering the situation in France in 1940 and beyond. Because of the reliance put in the defences of the Maginot Line, the French Army was outflanked and failed to hold up the German advance. During the four year occupation the French people had to endure great hardships.

Century 7 Quatrain 44

> *Then when a Bour will be very 'good'*
>
> *Carrying marks of justice,*
>
> *Bearing the oldest name of his line.*
>
> *He will be unjustly punished for his flight.*

This is a prediction of the fate of Louis XVI of France. The suggestion is that he was not as bad as sometimes painted. When the revolution forced him to be a constitutional monarch, he had to renounce his royal name, Bourbon. He tried to escape from France but was captured at Varennes in northeast France and taken back to Paris, where he met his violent end.

Century 7 Quatrain 80

The West free from the British Isles

The known one falls and then rises high

The sad Scottish rebel is not content

Then rebels even more and by warm night.

The West freeing itself from the British Isles signifies the American colonies and their fight for independence.

The rest of the quatrain tells of John Paul Jones, who was born in Scotland and eventually became a commander in the American Navy. He had great success against the British and after the revolutionary war he joined the Russian Navy as an Admiral and an advisor to Catherine the Great. He died as a disillusioned man in Paris.

Century 8

Century 8 Quatrain 1

> *Many will be confused by their wait,*
>
> *The people will be given no pardon:*
>
> *Who thought it better to wait,*
>
> *But they will not be given much pleasure*

There are conflicting opinions whether this is a genuine prophecy from Nostradamus or a fake. It would appear to deal with a lull or a time of waiting and could describe the 'phoney war'or 'before the German blitzkrieg of spring 1940'.

Century 8 Quatrain 2

Codom, Auch and the neighbourhood of Miroude,

Fire in the sky is seen around them,

The Sun and Mars joined in Leo and then Marmande,

Lightening, great hail and fallen walls in the Garonne.

All of the places mentioned are in the south west of France and what seems to be envisaged is a great catastrophe caused by unnatural weather. No clear timing is given.

Century 8 Quatrain 9

> *During the time the Eagle and the Cock are at Savona*
>
> *The Eastern Sea and Hungary will be united,*
>
> *The army at Naples, Palermo, the marches of Ancona*
>
> *Rome and Venice, there will be a horrible cry by the Barb.*

This appears to indicate events at the end of the Second World War in 1945. The allied forces are advancing through northern Italy and the Soviet armies have reached the Black Sea and Hungary. Barb is assumed to be Hitler railing against the failure of his Third Reich, which he claimed would last 1000 years.

Century 8 Quatrain 13

The brother crusader by unbettered love

By the use of Proetus will bring Bellerophon to death,

The fleet of 1,000 years, the ardent woman.

The potion taken both will die afterwards.

The British ship which took Napoleon to his final exile in St Helena was *H.M.S. Bellerophon*. Based on this fact, the quatrain seems to describe the end of the glory which Napoleon had known and the possible cause of his death.

Century 8 Quatrain 16

> *At the spot where Jason built his ship,*
>
> *There will be a flood so great and sudden,*
>
> *That it will not be possible to reach land,*
>
> *The wave will climb Mount Olympus.*

There is no real hint of timing in this quatrain but it points to a great flood disaster in the Aegean area which would effect Greece, the Balkans and Italy.

Century 8 Quatrain 17

A sudden demise of those living well,

Three brothers bring trouble to the world,

Enemies will take the city of the sea,

Famine, fire, blood, plague, double of every evil.

Nostradamus often gives warnings of trouble to come from vague enemies. These enemies could well be terrorists of one kind or another.

This warning is to those people in the world who have an easy life, probably in the north. The terrorists could come from three allied countries to the south, perhaps Islamic fundamentalists.

The city of the sea, could be any one of the major ports in the world.

Century 8 Quatrain 19

To support the great troubled cape,
The reds evil march to clear up the matter,
The family almost overwhelmed by death,
The red reds will strike the reds.

The mention of the cape in the first line probably alludes to King Louis XVI who, after the revolution, was known as citizen Capet. Discussion raged in the national convention between the reds (the moderates, and the red reds (the radicals) regarding the fate of the king. The radicals won and Louis XVI, Queen Marie Antoinette and the Dauphin were sent to their deaths.

Century 8 Quatrain 22

Gorsas, Narbonne, warning by salt,

Regarding the deception of the Paris promise,

The red city will not wish to agree

By the fleeing grey cloak, life is weakened.

The two men named in the first line were supporters of King Louis XVI who tried to contact him while he was in prison. The King had given on oath that he would not leave Paris. He broke this oath and tried to escape in the grey cloak of a Carmelite monk, only to be arrested again at Varennes and returned to Paris.

Century 8 Quatrain 28

> *The simulations of gold and silver are inflated,*
>
> *After the pillage discarded in the lake,*
>
> *At the realisation that all is lost,*
>
> *The scrips and lands are destroyed.*

The simulations of gold and silver surely refer to the wordings of the stock market. If that is the case, then this quatrain is predicting the great stock market crash of 1929.

Century 8 Quatrain 33

The great one will come from Verona and Vicenza,

He will have a name lacking dignity,

And will want to have vengeance in Venice,

He himself captured by the man of the sign.

Nostradamus often uses the names of towns to denote an area and Verona and Vicenza mean northern Italy.

This quatrain is about Mussolini who was born in northern Italy and he did not have a high-born name. Mussolini means 'maker of muslin'.

The second part of the verse seams to cover Mussolini's relationship with Hitler, who rescued him from his own people and controlled him completely at the end of World War II.

Century 8 Quatrain 37

> *The fortress close to the Thames*
>
> *Will fall when the king is imprisoned there*
>
> *Close to the bridge he will be seen in his shirt*
>
> *Facing death then shut in the fort.*

These are the facts surrounding the capture and execution of Charles I in January 1649. He was beheaded at Westminster and wore only his shirt for the execution.

Century 8 Quatrain 41

The fox elected without sounding a word,
Appearing a saint, living on bread alone,
After which he is a tyrant,
Putting his foot on the throats of the great.

This is a remarkable prophecy relating to Robespierre and calling him 'the fox', a name by which he was known two hundred years after the verse was written. During the French Revolution he gained total power in the Committee of Public Safety, only to have the tide turn against him in 1794, when he was denounced and guillotined.

Century 8 Quatrain 43

> *By the fall of two bastard things*
>
> *The nephew by blood will take the throne*
>
> *Inside lectoyre there will be arrow blows,*
>
> *The nephew will fearfully fold his standard.*

After the fall of two illegitimate regimes in France, the great nephew of Napoleon, Napoleon III, took the throne.

The word 'lectoyre' is an anagram for a suburb of Sedan where the French army was defeated by the Germans in 1870.

Century 8 Quatrain 50

The plague in the Capellades area,
Another famine near Sagunto,
The good old man's bastard knight
Will behead the great one of Tunis.

Nostradamus is looking ahead to famine and plague to come soon after his death.

The bastard knight is Don Juan of Austria who was the son of Charles V, Emperor of the Holy Roman Empire in 1573. Don Juan recaptured Tunis from the Algerian Corsairs and the inevitable end of their leader is forecast.

Century 8 Quatrain 53

> *At Boulogne he wants to atone for his mistakes,*
>
> *He cannot be at the temple of the Sun.*
>
> *He will fly to higher causes,*
>
> *He is one without equal.*

In 1804 Napoleon was in Boulogne with his Grand Army preparing to invade Britain.

It is thought that the temple of the Sun is a reference to London. The news of an attack in the east by the Russians and Austrians changed his plans and he moved his army to face this new threat, resulting in a successful campaign during the next few years.

Century 8 Quatrain 57

> *From a single soldier he will reach for empire,*
>
> *From a short robe he will take the long.*
>
> *Valiant in arms, but dangerous to the church,*
>
> *He will upset priests as water does the sponge.*

There has been much discussion about whether this verse refers to Napoleon or Cromwell.

The Cromwell allusion seems more direct. He was indeed a simple soldier who rose to take command and became Lord Protector.

Line two could predict that he studied at Oxford and graduated. He certainly did upset the clergy.

Century 8 Quatrain 60

> *The leaders of France and Romania,*
>
> *By sea and land with the English and Paris.*
>
> *Wonderful feats by this great host,*
>
> *The violent monster will lose Lorraine.*

This describes the wide-ranging alliances of the First World War and praises the victories of the Allies against the violent monster, Germany.

In the last line the prediction is made that Lorraine will be returned to France, having been lost to Germany in the Franco-Prussian war of 1870-71.

Century 8 Quatrain 64

Children transported in the Isles,
Two out of seven in despair,
The people will support this,
The hope of the leagues disappears.

A large number of British children were evacuated for their own safety from the cities to the countryside at the beginning of the Second World War. Some were even sent overseas to places such as Canada and Australia. The population supported this action, although it is easy to imagine the despair and anguish of parents and children.

The last line speaks of the failure of the League of Nations in avoiding the tragedy of the war.

Century 8 Quatrain 65

The old one defeated in his main hope,

He will become chief of his empire:

He will reign with grand power for twenty months,

A cruel tyrant, he will surrender power to one who is worse.

Nostradamus is again dealing with the Second World War.

After the defeat by Germany, the puppet Vichy regime in France was headed by a hero of the First World War, Marshal Petain. He was granted absolute powers by the French Assembly and ruled for twenty months. Now very old, he gave up his powers to his vice-premier, Pierre Naval, who was much more pro-German.

Century 8 Quatrain 70

> *The evil doer will emerge, bad and infamous,*
>
> *Tyrannizing Mesopotamiah:*
>
> *All friends are false friends,*
>
> *The land horrible and black.*

This is the emergence of Saddam Hussein in Iraq and the oppression which he has brought to this country. He has the tyrannical Shi'ites in the south and the Kurds in the north. He fought a desperate war against Iran and also invaded Kuwait. The horrible and black land is the result of the Gulf War of 1991 in both Iraq and Kuwait.

Century 8 Quatrain 76

> *More a butcher than king in England,*
>
> *Of humble birth, by force he will have an empire,*
>
> *Coward, with no faith, no law he will despoil the land,*
>
> *His time is so close that I sigh.*

Nostradamus seems to be returning to the consideration of Oliver Cromwell. He did indeed come from humble origins and he brought about the downfall of Charles I.

On winning the Civil War as leader of the Round- heads, he became Lord Protector.

The prophet sighs because of the closeness of Cromwell's time, which came less than a century after his own death.

Century 8 Quatrain 77

The third antichrist soon eliminated,

His war will last 27years:

The heretics are dead, captured or exiled

Blood, bodies, red water ravaging the earth.

Nostradamus refers regularly to three antichrists-Napoleon, Hitler and one still to afflict the world in the future.

The prophecy is vague regarding time and details, but it could be forecasting a future nuclear war which will devastate the earth and bring about Armageddon.

Century 8 Quatrain 80

> *The blood of the innocent, the widow and the virgin,*
>
> *Such great evil by the great Red:*
>
> *Holy icons burned*
>
> *No one can move for fear.*

The great Red can surely only be the Soviet dictator, Stalin. The Bolsheviks who led the Russian Revolution turned a great deal of their fury on the church and many churches and holy icons were destroyed. Countless millions were purged or sent to Siberian labour camps during Stalin's years in control and the population lived in constant fear.

Century 8 Quatrain 85

> *Between Bayonne and St Jean-de-Luz,*
>
> *The projection of Mars will be set:*
>
> *The actions of the northerner will extinguish the light.*
>
> *Then suffocation in bed without help.*

In 1814 the Duke of Wellington's army invaded France from Spain and camped at St Jean-de Luz. He then attacked the French forces at Bayonne.

The second part of the quatrain foresees the final defeat of Napoleon and his death in 1821.

Century 8 Quatrain 87

> *The plotted death will take place,*
>
> *Charged and the journey to death:*
>
> *Elected, confirmed, received and betrayed by his own,*
>
> *Innocent blood before faith by remorse.*

The death of Louis XVI was planned and plotted by the members of the National Convention.

The quatrain describes the trial and the king's journey to death on a tumbril through the streets of Paris. He had been both raised and condemned by his own people.

Century 8 Quatrain 92

> *Far outside the kingdom, taken on an hazardous journey,*
>
> *He will lead and hold a great army,*
>
> *The king will hold the nation captive,*
>
> *On his return he will pillage the whole country.*

There have been a few theories about the leader described in this quatrain, but the person who seems to fit the facts is Mao-Tse-Tung. He did lead the Chinese Communist Army on the Long March, thus saving the army from destruction at the hands of the Nationalist forces of Chiang Kai-Shek.

Following the final victory over the nationalists in 1949, Mao did dominate China and threw the country into confusion and repression in the late 1960's with the imposition of the Cultural Revolution.

Century 8 Quatrain 96

> *The sterile and fruitless synagogue*
>
> *Will be taken by the infidels:*
>
> *The daughter hunted by Babylon,*
>
> *Miserable and sad they will clip her wings.*

The temple of Solomon in Jerusalem would be taken by the Muslims and they would build their temple at that spot.

On many occassions, Nostradamus warns of a threat from Babylon, which is the Iraq of today. The verse suggests that Iraq will strike against Israel, which happened during the Gulf War of 1991 and could yet be a future development in the Middle East.

Century 8 Quatrain 99

By the power of three temporal kings,

Another place will be found for the sacred seat:

Whose spirit and body

Will be restored and acknowledged as the true See.

There have often been prophecies of the end of the Catholic Church as it is known today.

It is suggested here that the Holy See will have to be moved, perhaps because of the destruction of Rome by natural means or war. The new Holy See would be established and preside over a new era of goodness and holiness.

Century 9

Century 9 Quatrain 2

> *From the height of the Aventine hill, a voice can be heard,*
>
> *Withdraw, withdraw, all from both sides:*
>
> *The anger will be soothed by the blood of the reds,*
>
> *From Rimini and Prato, Colonna expelled.*

The beginning of this quatrain is interesting as it harks back to the time when members of the Roman Senate moved out to the Aventine hill to make a protest.
This probably relates to the situation in Italy when Mussolini took power and the opposition in protest boycotted the chamber. In 1945 the Italian communist partizans rose against the fascists and executed Mussolini and his mistress, thus soothing the anger felt at his takeover of government twenty one years before.

Century 9 Quatrain 7

Whoever opens the discovered tomb
And does not close it quickly:
Will be visited by evil unknown,
Better to be a Breton king or Norman.

In an attempt to ensure that his grave would not be disturbed, Nostradamus, as he was dying, requested his wife to have his body entombed upright in the wall of the church of the Cordeliers in Salon. During the French Revolution the grave was desecrated but later the remains were reburied in the present grave.

Century 9 Quatrain 11

The just man put wrongly to death,
He dies publically among them:
A great plague will visit this place,
So that the judges will be forced to flee.

Another reference to the execution of Louis XVI in Paris. As a committed monarchist, Nostradamus sees Louis as a just man and prophecies that his judges such as Robespierre and Saint Just, would suffer the same fate – public execution by guillotine.

Century 9 Quatrain 16

From Castille, Franco will leave the assembly,

The ambassador will not comply and causes a schism:

The followers of Rivera will be in the crowd,

And they will deny entry to the great gulf.

This quatrain is very unusual as it actually names Franco, the Spanish dicator, and his predecessor, Primo de Rivera. Rivera's son formed the Falange party which was later taken over by Franco. The Republican government had sent Franco to the Canary Islands but he returned surreptitiously to Spain, formed a military junta and plunged the country into a civil war. Franco was victorious and during the Second World War he kept Spain neutral and so denied Germany access through Spain to attack the very important British base in Gibraltar.

Century 9 Quatrain 20

> *By night he will pass through the forest of Reines,*
>
> *By a detour go two couples, the white stone:*
>
> *The king as a gray monk in Varennes*
>
> *The man called Capet causes a storm of fire and bloodletting.*

During the night of 20 June 1791, the King and Queen of France escaped from Paris in an attempt to reach the border. They did, indeed, pass through the forest of Reines and arrived at the town of Varennes, They did, however, raise suspicion in the town and were recaptured and taken back to Paris to face their fate.

Century 9 Quatrain 23

The second son outside under the trees,

The top of the arbour over his head ,

The father king is sad in the false temple,

He will concentrate the smoke of the meal as a sacrafice.

Following on quatrain 20, Louis XVI and his family have been brought back to Paris and are held in the Temple Prison. The sad scene depicted is the father in his lonely cell watching his younger son playing among the trees in the garden of the prison.

Century 9 Quatrain 28

> *The allied fleet to the port of Marseilles,*
>
> *In Venice to go to the Pannonias:*
>
> *Leaving the gulf and the Adriatic Sea,*
>
> *Devastation in Sicily, in Genoa cannon shots.*

During the Second World War, a decision was made to invade the south of France, instead of an advance through the Balkans, as favoured by some planners. The last line refers to the allied campaign in Sicily and the bombing of Genoa.

Century 9 Quatrain 31

The shaking of the earth at Mortara,

The islands of tin of St George are half sunk:

Lethargic from peace, the war will bring to life,

In the temple at Easter, cracks split wide.

This is a future prediciton of a huge earthquake which will affect a vast area from Mortara in Italy to the south west of England (the islands of tin of St George.)

There have been various prophecies of such a catastrophe, with a time suggested around the new millennium.

Let us hope that these are prophecies gone wrong!

Century 9 Quatrain 33

> *Hercules King of Rome and Annemark,*
>
> *One with the surname DeGaulle will lead France three times:*
>
> *Italy and St Mark will tremble,*
>
> *The acclaimed first monarch above all others.*

This prophecy seems to point unneringly to Charles de Gaulle, who led France three times. From 1940 he led the Free French in London and after the liberation of France in 1944, he headed a provisional government until resigning in 1946.He was called back from retirement in 1958 and was president of the new fifth Republic from 1959 until 1969.

Century 9 Quatrain 37

Bridges and mills destroyed in December,

The Garonne will rise very high:

Walls and buildings in Toulouse brought down,

No-one will know his place before a midwife.

This is another dire prophecy telling of floods and earthquakes in south west France. This is a disaster still to happen and this quatrain joins the other predictions of calamity due to befall the human race in the not too distant future.

Prophecies have been wrong!

Century 9 Quatrain 48

> *The great oceanic city,*
>
> *Encircled by crystal:*
>
> *In the winter and the spring,*
>
> *Will be tried by a terrible wind.*

Yet prediction of climate change and how it will affect the new skyscraper cities of the world. The city referred to could be New York, Hong Kong or some such modern city on the coast.

It has been predicted that with the warming of the oceans, typhoons and hurricanes will increase in ferocity and this could well affect the modern high rise cities.

Century 9 Quatrain 49

Ghent and Brussels will move against Antwerp,

The London parliament will put their king to death,

The salt and wine will bring him down,

These things will bring confusion to the kingdom.

The first line appears to foresee the changes in Holland as the result of the end of the war with Spain in 1648. The following year the English parliament beheaded King Charles I.

The mention of salt and wine is referring to the taxation imposed by Charles and was one of the factors in his downfall.

Century 9 Quatrain 55

> *The horrible war planned by the West*
>
> *Will be followed in a year by plague,*
>
> *So terrible, affecting young, old and animals;*
>
> *Blood, fire, Mercury, Mars, Jupiter in France.*

The conjunction of planets forecast here is a fairly regular occurrence and, therefore, the prediction can fit various times. A major war is being forecast for the end of this century or just after and the plague could well be AIDS which could be the world's greatest risk to health, apart from wars.

Century 9 Quatrain 63

Wailing and tears, cries and great yells,
Nera Narbonne, at Bayonne and in Foix:
Oh what horrible changing calamities,
Before Mars revolves several times .

This seems to reflect the turmoil, violence and confusion in the south west of France during the French Revolution.

The reference to Mars could be referring to the arrival of the British Army under the Duke of Wellington from Spain and the fighting around Bayonne and St Jean-de-Luz in 1814.

The terrible changes which so upset Nostradamus would also include the elevation of his Antichrist Napoleon to the post of First Consul of France.

Century 9 Quatrain 65

> *He will make his way to the moon,*
>
> *Where he will find himself in foreign land,*
>
> *The unripe fruit will make a great shame,*
>
> *Much ranting and great praise.*

Here the prophet is forecasting man's landing on the moon and perhaps even, in time, setting up a colony there in a strange environment.

This is a remarkable prophecy when one considers that the first flights into space only began about ten years before the actual landing in 1969.

Century 9 Quatrain 68

> *From the mountain Amar will erase the noble,*
>
> *The evil will take place where the Saone and the Rhone meet*
>
> *The woods hide soldiers on St Lucy's Day,*
>
> *What tree has hidden such a horrible throne.*

This verse foresees the Reign of Terror which followed the execution of Louis XVI. The town of Lyons is situated where the rivers Saone and Rhone meet, and it was here that a dreadful massacre took place. Lyons had been loyal to Louis and the retaliation of the the republicans was vicious and destructive.

Lines three and four of the quatrain foresee the defeat of a Royalist army by the Republicans on St Lucy's Day, 13 December 1793.

Century 9 Quatrain 77

> *The fallen realm will convict the convict the King*
>
> *Jurors drawn by lot sentence the Queen to death,*
>
> *The Queen's son also denied life,*
>
> *The consort's fate shared by the mistress.*

Nostradamus again returns to his vision of the greatest event in France on his future horizons – the Revolution . Some months after the execution of the King, his Queen Marie Antoinette was also sent to the guillotine, apparently after a trial using jurors drawn by lot. Madame du Barry, the mistress of the grandfather of the king was also executed and the 11 year- old Dauphin died in prison.

Century 9 Quatrain 86

From Bourg-la-Reine they will stretch to Chartres,

And will be near Pont d'Antony,

The seven for peace are clever as birds,

Their army will enter a sealed Paris.

After the battle of Waterloo and at the end of Napoleon's attempt to take back power, the nations ranged against him entered a Paris which was almost an open city. The seven nations for peace were Britain, Russia, Spain,Portugal, Austria, Sweden and Prussia. The French army was in retreat and took up position along the Loire.

Century 9 Quatrain 89

> *Fortune will prosper Philip for seven years,*
>
> *He will lay low the Arabs,*
>
> *Then in the middle, a strange affair,*
>
> *The young one will reduce his strength.*

Louis Philippe, Duc d'Orleans overthrew King Charles X of France in 1830 and for seven years he brought peace and prosperity to the country. In these years he also conquered Algeria, bringing further success.

After this period public opinion turned against him and rioting flared up over voting rights. This discontent led to the nephew of Napoleon Bonaparte first becoming president in 1848 and then emperor in 1852 as Napoleon III.

Century 9 Quatrain 90

A captain of Greater Germany,

Will bring deceitful succour,

A King of King help from Hungary

His uprising will bring great bloodshed.

Hitler maded great play of the term Greater Germany and his plans for its establishment and expansion . He was indeed aided by the regime in Hungary and great bloodshed was visited on the German people and allthe peoples of Europe.

Century 9 Quatrain 98

> *The suffering caused by a single person,*
>
> *The agent of the opposing party,*
>
> *He will command force against the Lyonnais,*
>
> *They will be subjected to the great warlord.*

This is another verse about the repression of the royalists in Lyons in 1793. The Committee of Public Safety ordered the attack and the city's defences and the homes of the royalists were destroyed and many thousands were killed.

Century 9 Quatrain 100

> *There will be a night naval battle,*
>
> *Destruction in the West, fire to the ships:*
>
> *The new custom colours the great ship,*
>
> *The defeated are angry, the victory in the rain.*

In 1588 the Spanish suffered a humiliating defeat by the English when their powerful Armada was scattered and largely destroyed.

This quatrain describes the attack by fire ships on the Spanish fleet at Calais and the subsequent bombardment by the English under Sir Francis Drake. The Armada had to sail and a gale drove the ships into the North Sea. The defeat of the Armada extinguished the threat of a Spanish invasion of England.

Century 10

Century 10 Quatrain 1

> *To the enemy, the enemy promises faith*
>
> *That the captives will not be held:*
>
> *Captured, near death, with only their shirts,*
>
> *The remainder are damned by being sustained.*

In this quatrain Nostradamus appears to be peering into the future of the countless number of prisoners of war created by the centuries of warfare stretching ahead of his own time.

All wars have produced atrocites committed against prisoners, but none worse than the Second World War. One only has to think of the prisoners of the Japanese in the far east, Russian prisoners of the Germans on the eastern front in Europe and, likewise, the German prisoners of the Russians.

Century 10 Quatrain2

The sail of the galley will be hidden,

The large fleet will flee from the smaller:

Ten ships will force it to turn,

A great defeat for the united faith.

This verse returns to the prediction of the defeat of the Spanish Armada by the English fleet. The large fleet is the Armada with its formidable galleons and the smaller is the English smaller but more manoevrable ships. The Armada was scattered by the fireships and the gales and so was defeated the dream of PhilipII of Spain to bring England back to the Catholic faith.

Century 10 Quatrain 4

> *On the stroke of midnight the army chief*
>
> *Will save himself disappearing abruptly:*
>
> *Seven years later his fame undiminished,*
>
> *His return will be acclaimed.*

Charles II fled after his defeat at the battle of Worcester in 1651 and eventually escaped to France.

Seven years later Oliver Cromwell died and public opinion swung again towards the monarchy.

Two years after the death of Cromwell, Charles was received back to the throne, with acclamation.

Century 10 Quatrain 10

Stained by murder and great adulteries,

Great enemy of all mankind:

He will be worse than his grandfathers, uncles or fathers,

Hell, fire, water, blood and inhumanity.

This is a very fierce condemnation of an enemy of all mankind. There are many theories regarding the object of this tirade, but the most likely is Napoleon, who was Nostradamus' first Antichrist. Napoleon certainly caused complete turmoil throughout Europe.

Century 10 Quatrain 12

> *Elected Pope, he will be mocked by his electors,*
>
> *Quick and shy, suddenly quietened:*
>
> *His goodness and kindness will provoked his death,*
>
> *Their fear leads to his death in the night.*

Nostradamus returns once again to the strange happenings in the Vatican surrounding the death of Pope John Paul I.

Elected Pope in August 1978, he died in September 1978, the second shortest reign in the history of the Catholic church. John Paul I was known to be determined to root out abuses of power at the centre of the church and there have always been theories that he was, in fact, murdered.

Century 10 Quatrain 16

Happy reigning in France, happy with life,

No knowledge of blood, death, fury and rape,

Envied not only by flatterers,

A protected king with much faith in the kitchen.

These lines refer to King Louis XVIII of France following the death in prison of his nephew, Louis XVII, he was king in name from 1795 and in fact after the overthrow of Napoleon. He had a relatively carefree life, did not occupy himself enough with public affairs and was overfond of his food and drink.

Century 10 Quatrain 22

> *Not wishing to agree to separation,*
>
> *He who later will be considered unworthy,*
>
> *The King of the Isles will be removed by force,*
>
> *In his place one not marked for a king.*

This prophecy appears to fit perfectly with the circumstances of the abdication of Edward VIII of Great Britain. He was in love with the American divorcee Wallis Simpson and wished to make her his queen. When the establishment of the day made it clear that this would not be accepted, he gave up the crown and went into exile.

His brother, the Duke of York, succeeded him and, although not marked out as King, became the greatly loved George VI.

Century 10 Quatrain 23

> *Protests are made to the ungrateful people,*
>
> *The army will take Antibes,*
>
> *In the arch of Monaco will be cries of grief,*
>
> *And at Frejus the other shore will be seized.*

In 1944 the allied invasion of the south of France took place involving mainly American and Free French forces. The main landings were made at Frejus and St Raphael and the troops then advanced east towards Monaco, west towards Marseilles and inland to the north.

Century 10 Quatrain 32

> *Each year the great empire will last,*
>
> *One on the others will come to create it:*
>
> *But his reign and life will be but for a short time,*
>
> *His ships will enable him to continue for two years.*

Hitler's Third Reich was all powerful until 1943, when it began to crumble. His armies were driven back from Stalingrad, El Alamein and the rest of North Africa. The Russians began their inexorable drive towards Germany and the British and Americans advanced up Italy and landed in Normandy. He lasted only two more years with only a few successes at sea.

Century 10 Quatrain 34

> *The empire of Gaul held together by war,*
>
> *He will be betrayed by his brother-in-law*
>
> *He will ride a wild horse,*
>
> *The acts of the brother-in-law will be long hated.*

This would fit another allusion to Napoleon. The Emperor held his empire together during fourteen years of warfare and Joaquim Muŕat, King of Naples, was one of his greatest generals. Murat was married to Napoleon's sister Caroline and he did, eventually, plot against Napoleon.

Century 10 Quatrain 36

> *After the king speaking of wars,*
>
> *The United Isle will hold him in contempt:*
>
> *Some good years of foraging and pillaging*
>
> *The tyranny changing prices on the island.*

Could this refer to the contempt in which the people of the United Isle of Britain held Hitler?

He did indeed have some good years of conquest and victories before the allies turned the tide against his Third Reich in the Second World War.

The mention of price control on the island could also indicate the rationing which had to be endured during Hitler's attempt to starve Britain into submission.

Century 10 Quatrain 40

The young heir to the throne of Britain,

Approved by his dying father,

On whose death London will take issue,

And demanding the realm from his son.

This is another quatrain which prophecies the abdication of Edward VIII. The wording of the verse would appear to be sympathetic to Edward and his love for Wallis Simpson, but the vision of Nostradamus may be clouded by the mists of the intervening four hundred years.

Century 10 Quatrain 47

> *From Bruges to Giurlaine,*
>
> *They will bear down on treason:*
>
> *The great prelate of Leon through Formentera,*
>
> *They will act against false pilgrims and destroyers.*

During the Spanish Civil War, Franco set up his military junta in Burgos and the verse refers to various actions, including the Republican attack on Formentera which took place. Some of the allusions are difficult to understand, although, in the eyes of Nostradamus, the false pilgrims could be the communists on the Republican side.

Century 10 Quatrain 49

Garden of the world close to the new city,
On the road of the hollow mountains:
Taken and plunged into the Vat,
Forcably drinking poisoned water.

It is difficult to relate this verse to anything which has happened in past history. It probably has something to say for our time or for the future.

If one assumes that the hollow mountains are skyscrapers seen from the distance of over four hundred years, then the new city is almost certainly New York and it is interesting to note that across the Hudson River is New Jersey- which is called the Garden State.

The actions described appears to be terrorist attacks.

Century 10 Quatrain 55

> *The unfortunate marriage will be celebrated*
>
> *In great joy, but have an unhappy ending:*
>
> *The husband and mother will have disdain for the daughter-in-law,*
>
> *The dead Apollo and the more wretched daughter-in-law.*

If this quatrain is applied to the present day, it makes a remarkable prophecy. The marriage of the Prince and Princess of Wales took place with high hopes and caused great joy in the nation. It ended in unhappiness and great acrimony and no doubt Prince Charles and the Queen viewed Diana and her subsequent lifestyle with disdain. The unexpected and tragic death of the Princess in 1997 adds poignancy to the prophecy.

Century 10 Quatrain 57

The exalted one will not recognise his sceptre,

Disgrace for the young children of the greatest:

There has never been a more rotten or cruel one,

The black one will send their husbands to their death.

Could this deal with the third Antichrist of Nostradamus and could he be Saddam Hussein of Iraq?

If this line is taken, this verse comfortably covers the fate of the two sons-in-law of Saddam. The two men defected to the West with their wives and families but eventually returned to Iraq, hoping for forgiveness from Saddam. In the event the daughters of Saddam Hussein divorced their husbands, who were killed along with other members of their family.

Century 10 Quatrain 64

Lament Milan, Lament Lucca and Florence,

Your great leader goes up on the chariot,

Changing the government as the advance nears Venice,

While changes will be made in Rome.

The government of the Duce of Italy, Mussolini, fell in 1944 and until the end of the Second World War in 1945 he headed up a puppet regime supported by Germany. All of the towns and cities mentioned in the verse suffered from bombing or involvement in the bitter fighting of the Italian campaign.

Century 10 Quatrain 65

Oh great Rome, your ruin is coming,

Not of your walls, but your body and blood:

The man of letters will wound badly,

The point of iron put to all at the sleeve.

Nostradamus returns many times to what he sees as the punishment which the church of Rome will have to bear for many sins committed.

In recent times there have been many criticisms of the church, including its attitude during the Second World War and the dealings of the Vatican Bank. It would appear that the prophet foresees many of the attacks coming from writers and academics.

Century 10 Quatrain 67

> *An earthquake so strong in the month of May,*
>
> *Saturn, Capricorn, Jupiter, Mercury in Taurus:*
>
> *Venus also Cancer, Mars in Virgo,*
>
> *Hail larger then an egg will fall.*

Nostradamus has forecast the end of the world for the year 3797AD and this prophecy of great natural upheaval could take place not long before that date.

Century 10 Quatrain 69

The shining action of the old one is praised anew,

They will be so great in south and north:

His own sister raised many,

A murderous flight in the maquis of Ambellon.

It is likely that the old one referred to is Marshal Petain who, in 1940, was made head of the German puppet Vichy government in France. Petain had been a great hero of the First World War and was revered by the people. He was eventually seen as only a figurehead and after the liberation he was tried for treason.

Those who were great in the south and the north were the members of the Resistance. After the landings in Normandy in 1944, the Resistance became very active and tied down large numbers of German troops, thus aiding the allied advance. Many units of the Maquis suffered heavy casualties at that time.

Century 10 Quatrain 72

In the year 1999 in the seventh month,

From the sky will come a great king of terror.

The great King of the Mongols will return

Before and afterwards Mars will rule with great happiness.

Having survived the dreaded date of July 1999 we can say that this prophecy has not been fulfilled. Perhaps Nostradamus' only mistake was being too specific with the date.

There have often been warnings of the danger to Western civilisation of the rise of China and of another Ghengis Khan emerging and leading his army westwards. The final line does, however, suggest and era of peace and happiness to follow this threat and this could happen early in the 21st century with the coming of the Age of Aquarius. This is surely a hopeful thought with which to end this most famous doomsday forecast from the prophet.

Century 10 Quatrain 75

The one so much awaited will never return

Inside Europe, in Asia he will appear:

One born from great Hermes,

And he will grow greater than all the kings of the East.

Here Nostradamus is dealing with the emergence of a great new spiritual leader and he appears to be prophecying that the long awaited return of Jesus Christ will not happen. He says that this leader will come from the east and will bear a different message from that of Jesus Christ.

This is a good example of a coded forecast as he would have been burned as a heretic if it had been understood in his own time.

Century 10 Quatrain 82

Cries, lamentation and tears will come from all sides

Pretending to flee they will make a last attack:

Surrounding the parks will be established deep platforms,

Refused by violence and murdered.

This describes a battle which flows one way and then another. It could be a feint before a concerted attack or it could be a counter-attack mounted after the arrival of fresh forces. Some interpreters place the battle during the Napoleonic Wars but the description could fit many of the battles fought during the First and Second World Wars.

Century 10 Quatrain 83

The signal for the battle will not be given,

Thy will be forced to leave the park:

The ensign will be seen around Ghent,

Of the one who will put his own to death.

This is similar to the previous quatrain, but this time specific mention is made of Ghent, or Flanders. Again, artillery parks are involved. Countless battles have been fought over Flanders fields through the centuries but the ones which seem to fit are those in the First and Second World Wars.

Century 10 Quatrain 86

> *The King of Europe will come like a griffin,*
>
> *The ones from the north with,*
>
> *From reds and white him will be led a great army,*
>
> *And they will confront the King of Babylon.*

This points to a great struggle by the Europeans and Americans against Babylon or Iraq. It could refer to the Gulf War of 1991 or perhaps a future confrontation.

Century 10 Quatrain 88

Foot and horse on the eve
Will make an overwhelming entry by sea:
The port of Marseilles will be entered,
Tears, cries and blood, never a time so bitter.

This is a very good portrayal of the landings of the mainly American force in the south of France in 1944. After establishing a successful bridgehead, the first major target was Marseilles and the liberation of the city was carried out by the Free French forces.

Century 10 Quatrain 89

> *From brick to marble the walls will be altered,*
> *Fifty seven years of peace:*
> *Joyful people, the aqueduct renewed,*
> *Health, great fruitfulness and mellow times.*

During the reign of Louis XIV of France, the country experienced 57 years without internal strife and energies were employed in building another improvements. The change from brick to marble suggests the creation of the Palace of Versailles and the mention of the aqueduct could foresee the construction of canals which took place at that time.

Century 10 Quatrain 90

The inhuman tyrant will die 100 times,

An educated and debonair man takes his place,

All of the senate under his hand,

He will be upset by a cunning and reckless man.

Once again, Nostradamus sees his Antichrist, Napoleon,but now he has been exiled to St Helena and his place taken by Louis XVIII who was known as Le Debonnaire. One can imagine the sadness and frustration of the former emperor, removed from the centre of power.

Century 10 Quatrain 95

> *A very powerful king will enter Spain,*
> *Conquering the south by land and sea:*
> *This evil one will crush the crescent,*
> *Lowering the wings of those of Friday.*

The prophet is looking ahead over 200 years from his own time and sees the all-conquering Napoleon who has annexed Spain and Italy and has continued to expand his empire.

The reference to the crushing of the crescent and 'those of Friday' acknowledges his victories over the Muslims in the battles at Cairo and Aboukir.

Century 10 Quatrain 99

The end of the wolf lion, bull and ass

The timid deer will be with the hounds

The sweet Manna will no longer drop on them

More vigilance and restraint for the hounds.

This verse surely cannot be forecasting the demise of all the animals mentioned.

There can be various interpretations,but the most likely is that these different beasts represent the nations of Europe which are giving up many of their purely national powers and moving to an ever closer union in our time.

Century 10 Quatrain 100

England will create a great empire,
All-powerful for more than 3 centuries:
Great forces will move by land and sea,
The Portugese will not be pleased.

This is a remarkably correct prophecy. The English Empire and then the British Empire began to be established in the early 17th century and lasted until midway through the 20th century, when it disintegrated, mainly due to the Second World War.

The Empire is now a loose family of nations called The Commonwealth, which still acknowledges the Queen of Britain as its head.

The Portugese were also empire builders and no doubt they were not too happy to observe the growth of wealth and power which the Empire brought to Britain.